PINK FLOYD

PINK FLOYD

SONG BY SONG

ANDREW WILD

FONTHILL

This one is for Beany and Darno, who planted the seed,
For Nick, who watered it,
And for Cliff, who still allows it to flower.

Fonthill Media Language Policy

Fonthill Media publishes in the international English language market. One language edition is published worldwide. As there are minor differences in spelling and presentation, especially with regard to American English and British English, a policy is necessary to define which form of English to use. The Fonthill Policy is to use the form of English native to the author. Andrew Wild was born and educated in the United Kingdom; therefore British English has been adopted in this publication.

Fonthill Media Limited
Fonthill Media LLC
www.fonthillmedia.com
office@fonthillmedia.com

First published in the United Kingdom and the United States of America 2017

British Library Cataloguing in Publication Data:
A catalogue record for this book is available from the British Library

ISBN 978-1-78155-599-6

Typeset in 10.5pt on 13pt MinionPro
Printed and bound in England

Acknowledgements

To Amanda, Rosie, and Amy, who are my everything.

To my besties: Jules, Graeme, Lee, Damian, Horse, Nick, and Pongo, and their much-better halves Lisa, Sally, Nicola, Chris, Jenny, Chris, and Suze.

Hearty nods go out to Cliff, Stacy, and the team at Progzilla Radio—the UK's only dedicated twenty-four–seven prog station. Listen now at progzilla.com, or delve through the archives at andrewwild.progzilla.com.

My thanks to Stephen Lambe, Emma Roebuck, Jezz Palmer, and Jay Slater.

My grateful thanks also to my proof-reader Anthony Rowsick (he's American) and to Jules Cox, photographer to the Rainow elite. Top men.

CONTENTS

Introduction

If 'dancing is the vertical expression of a horizontal desire', as George Bernard Shaw is alleged to have said, then music, by extension, must be seen as a trigger for romance, love, and sex.

Yet, there are other emotions elicited by music—anger, isolation, regret, dismay, fear.

Pink Floyd did not write about sex, love, and romance; they wrote about anger, isolation, regret, dismay, and fear. These themes, not always obvious starting points in popular music, were married to a rare dynamism in rock music. Pink Floyd's best work—'Interstellar Overdrive'; 'A Saucerful of Secrets'; 'Careful with That Axe, Eugene'; 'Set the Controls for the Heart of the Sun', 'Atom Heart Mother'; 'Echoes'; 'Us and Them'; 'The Great Gig in the Sky'; 'Shine on You Crazy Diamond'; 'Dogs'; 'Mother'; 'Hey You'; 'Comfortably Numb'; 'The Final Cut'; and 'Marooned'—combine musical passages of quiet reflection with aggressive louder sections, usually embroidered by technically proficient and vibrant instrumental soloing. This rise and fall, build and release, escalation and climax created tensions and responses that can certainly be analysed as being more physical than rational.

Crucially, Pink Floyd were English and middle class. No one does repressed angst quite like the English middle classes, and in Roger Waters they had a lyricist who could portray in vivid language the drawbacks of privilege, the vagaries of fame, the greed of big business, and the depression of post-war life—the clinical expressions of the shortcomings of middle class desire, if you like.

There have been many books written about Pink Floyd, but none that cover the band's entire pukka oeuvre from 'Arnold Layne' to 'Louder than Words'. With the band's story seemingly concluded, it seems right to evaluate their entire recording career, and to look again at the songs that led to Pink Floyd becoming the third bestselling band of all time.

Pink Floyd's most successful period critically and musically—the eight albums from 1970 to 1983—combine the pithy lyrics of Roger Waters, the soulful voice and often breathtaking guitar solos of David Gilmour, and, until 1979, the jazz-influenced piano and keyboard abilities of the late Richard Wright. Together these three wrote the band's best work, usually in combinations of twos and threes, but also individually. When working together as equals, the three principals of Pink Floyd were significantly more than the sum of their individual strengths.

However, in truth, Pink Floyd were never able to shake off the ghost of their original singer and songwriter, the late Syd Barrett. While there is almost no trace of Barrett's direct musical influence on *The Dark Side of the Moon*, *Wish You Were Here*, or *The Wall*, his fall from grace and slide into insanity colours all three of these significant—and massively selling—albums.

Pink Floyd: Song By Song discusses every track on every Pink Floyd studio album, together with those songs such as 'Arnold Layne', which were originally released on singles. It looks at the stories behind the songs, their context within the parent albums, the times they were written and recorded in, and when they were played live.

Listening again to the entire Pink Floyd catalogue in preparation for this book has been a surprise—it has some years since I listened to *More* and *A Momentary Lapse of Reason,* and it may be some considerable time before I voluntarily repeat the exercise. But when this band was on form, and they barely put a foot wrong between *Atom Heart Mother* and *The Final Cut* —with flashes of inspiration both before and after—they were, indeed, more than mere ordinary men.

Andrew Wild
Rainow, Cheshire
April 2017

1

Floyd Phase 1: 1965–1968 Lose Your Mind and Play

Before *Piper* (1965–1967)

Much has been written about the history of Pink Floyd, and those wishing to read excellent accounts are directed to drummer Nick Mason's memoirs *Inside Out: A Personal History of Pink Floyd*, Mark Blake's wonderfully readable *Pigs Might Fly: The Inside Story of Pink Floyd* (published as *Comfortably Numb* in the US), and Glenn Povey's definitive *Echoes: The Complete History of Pink Floyd*.

The facts are these. Architecture students Roger Waters and Nick Mason met in 1963 at the London Polytechnic. Their first band together, Sigma 6, was formed in late 1963 with singer Keith Noble, bassist Clive Metcalfe, and keyboard player (and occasional guitarist) Richard Wright. Guitarist Rado 'Bob' Klose joined in September 1964, and the band went through several names—including the Meggadeaths, the Abdabs and the Screaming Abdabs, Leonard's Lodgers, and the Spectrum Five—before settling on the Tea Set. In late 1964, Metcalfe and Noble left to form their own band, and guitarist Syd Barrett, a childhood friend of singer Chris Dennis and Waters, joined in their place. Dennis, a technician with the RAF, was posted to Bahrain in early 1965 and so Barrett became the band's frontman; he then took over lead guitar when Klose quit the band in mid-1965. The group first referred to themselves as the Pink Floyd Sound in late 1965, when another band called Tea Set were on the same bill. By 1966, the group's repertoire consisted mainly of rhythm and blues, and they acquired managers Peter Jenner and Andrew King after being seen by Jenner at a performance at the Marquee Club in March. The group became part of London's underground music scene, performing Barrett's original songs and experimenting with long instrumentals and light shows.

> At the end of 1966, a combination of timing and luck was starting to work for us and with Syd's distinctive song-writing and our improvisational style we did have a rather rough but definitely original musical approach to offer the record companies.
>
> Nick Mason, *Inside Out: A Personal History of Pink Floyd* (2004)

When Pink Floyd signed to EMI records in February 1967, they had already recorded their debut single.

'Arnold Layne'

Syd Barrett: lyrics, music, guitars, vocals
Richard Wright: Farfisa organ, vocals
Roger Waters: bass
Nick Mason: drums

Recorded 29 January 1967 at Sound Techniques Studios, London, and released on 11 March 1967.

Pink Floyd's debut single, Syd Barrett's 'Arnold Layne', was privately recorded on 29 January 1967 at Sound Techniques Studios in Chelsea. Sound Techniques was one of London's foremost independent studios in the 1960s and early 1970s. The sessions were produced by Joe Boyd, who had previously recorded Pink Floyd at Sound Techniques for the soundtrack to the documentary film *Tonite Let's All Make Love in London*, and would go on to produce classic albums for the likes of Fairport Convention, Nick Drake, and John Martyn.

Unreleased renditions of 'Matilda Mother', 'Chapter 24', and 'Interstellar Overdrive' were also recorded in these same sessions, along with 'Candy and a Currant Bun', the B-side of 'Arnold Layne'.

> We were recommended to Sound Techniques. Can't remember who by, but they hadn't been open very long. I think we were one of the first groups to use it, but a lot now go there because of our success.
>
> Richard Wright, quoted in *Beat International* (September 1967)

The song was Barrett's LSD-inspired rewrite of a story told to him by Roger Waters: that women's underwear would go missing from the washing line of his mother's house in Cambridge after she started taking in lodgers. It took Syd three weeks to perfect the imagery and rhymes.[1]

An attempt to re-cut 'Arnold Layne' at EMI on 27 February did not improve upon the earlier version, and Boyd's Sound Techniques recording was used for the debut single. Some sources suggest that the song was recorded on 27 February at Sound Techniques, but this seems unlikely.

> We knew we wanted to be rock'n'roll stars and we wanted to make singles, so it seemed the most suitable song to condense into 3 minutes without losing too much.
>
> Nick Mason, as quoted in *The Piper at the Gates of Dawn* by John Cavanagh (2003)

> I listened to it a couple of times and discovered that it was good.
>
> Syd Barrett, as quoted in *The Herald* (15 March 1967)

Sung in a resolutely English accent, and touching on a determinedly English eccentricity, 'Arnold Layne' was entirely without precedent. It can almost be regarded as a turning point in '60s pop: when the UK was finally able to create wholly original music on its own terms.

The first known live performance of 'Arnold Layne' was on 6 March 1967, a few days before the single was released. 'Arnold Layne' was played sporadically throughout the rest of 1967. It was sound-checked by the band during the 1987–1989 concert tour, but never performed in public. 'Arnold Layne' was subsequently performed on David Gilmour's solo tour in 2006, sung by Richard Wright or, on one occasion, by David Bowie. Fittingly, 'Arnold Layne' proved to be the last song ever performed on stage by Pink Floyd. The performance at The Barbican, London, on 10 May 2007 featured Gilmour, Mason, and Wright, with Jon Carin (keyboards, vocals) and Andy Bell (bass), and was the finale of *The Madcap's Last Laugh*, a tribute show for Syd Barrett.

'Candy and a Currant Bun'

Syd Barrett: lyrics, music, guitars, vocals
Richard Wright: Farfisa organ, vocals
Roger Waters: bass, vocals
Nick Mason: drums, vocals

Recorded 29 January 1967, at Sound Techniques Studios, London and released on 11 March 1967 as the B-side of 'Arnold Layne'.

B-sides in the 1960s were often as interesting as the more commercial songs they were helping to promote—think of 'Rain' by the Beatles, 'The Spider and the Fly' by the Rolling Stones, or 'Gloria' by Them.

'Candy and a Currant Bun' was recorded at Sound Techniques during the same sessions as 'Arnold Layne'. An EMI acetate has alternative lyrics, a different verse structure, and no organ or guitar solos.

Whereas both 'Arnold Layne' and its follow-up 'See Emily Play' would have sat uncomfortably on *The Piper at the Gates of Dawn*, 'Candy and a Currant Bun' would have fitted in right alongside 'Lucifer Sam', 'Matilda Mother' and 'Flaming'. The instrumental section is surely a brief indication of how exciting the band's live shows would have been at the time.

> 'Candy and a Currant Bun' was originally called 'Let's Roll Another One', including the lyric 'I'm high, don't try to spoil my fun.' Since this was deemed to be pushing our

luck [with] the still very conservative record industry, a complete alternative set of lyrics had to be cobbled together.

Nick Mason, *Inside Out: A Personal History of Pink Floyd* (2004)

One of Syd's great fractured masterpieces.

Cliff Jones, *Echoes* (1996)

Performed live as early as September 1966 under its original title, the first known live performance as 'Candy and a Currant Bun' was at the Playhouse Theatre, London, on 3 April 1967. The last was at the Savile Theatre, London, on 1 October 1967.

'See Emily Play'

Syd Barrett: lyrics, music, guitars, vocals
Richard Wright: Farfisa organ, piano, harpsichord, vocals
Roger Waters: bass, vocals
Nick Mason: drums

Recorded 23 May 1967, at Sound Techniques Studios, London and released on 16 June 1967.

The follow-up to 'Arnold Layne', 'See Emily Play' was written specifically for a concert event ('Games for May') in London on 12 May 1967. Their set-list that evening comprised most of *The Piper at the Gates of Dawn*, then being recorded at EMI Studios. Nine days later, Pink Floyd recorded 'See Emily Play' at Sound Techniques, after several abortive attempts at Abbey Road in the preceding few days.

Future member David Gilmour was present at these sessions, but did not perform on the song. Gilmour was shocked by his old friend Syd Barrett's appearance.

Syd rang me up and asked me along to the studio. When I got there he gave me a complete blank. I'll go on record as saying that was when he changed. He was one of the great rock and roll tragedies.

David Gilmour, quoted in *Melody Maker* (19 May 1973)

The resultant recording, 'the perfect amalgam of psychedelic excess and pure pop', would be released as a single on 16 June 1967.[2, 3] Reaching a high of number six in the chart dated 26 July 1967, it would sit comfortably next to such 'summer of love' songs as 'All You Need Is Love' (The Beatles, no. 1), 'Alternate Title' (The Monkees, no. 4), 'A Whiter Shade of Pale' (Procol Harum, no. 7), 'Here Come the Nice' (Small Faces, no. 18), 'Strange Brew' (Cream, no. 29), and 'Paper Sun' (Traffic, no. 32).

> 'See Emily Play' was a perfect exemplar of the influences wafting from Britain from the American West Coast being rewired into a very English sense of fairy-tale innocence.
>
> John Harris, *The Dark Side of the Moon: The Making of Pink Floyd's Masterpiece* (2005)

As a subtle tribute to Barrett, part of the vocal melody of 'See Emily Play' was played on by Richard Wright at the very end of 'Shine on You Crazy Diamond Part IX' (from 12:10 to 12:15).

The first live performance of 'See Emily Play' was at the Games for May concert at the Queen Elizabeth Hall in London on 12 May 1967. It was performed on occasion throughout 1967. A live version, recorded in Stockholm on 10 December 1967, was released on *The Early Years 1965–1972* in 2016; however, despite a pleasingly heavier arrangement from the band, Syd's vocals are utterly inaudible.

'Lucy Leave' / 'I'm a King Bee'

These two songs were long available on bootlegs, and were officially released in 2015 as part of the very limited twin vinyl single *1965: Their First Recordings*. These were once attributed to a November 1966 session at Thompson Private Recorders in Hemel Hempstead, but date from much earlier—December 1964 to January 1965. 'Lucy Leave' is a bouncing slice of R&B with some thrillingly ragged lead guitar, while 'I'm A King Bee' is a slow blues shuffle, a polite version of the Slim Harpo song recorded by The Rolling Stones on their debut album in 1964.

'Double O Bo' / 'Remember Me' / 'Walk with Me Sydney' / 'Butterfly'

Four more songs from early 1965 not heard publicly, or even widely known about, until they were given a very limited release as two 7-inch vinyl records in 2015. 'Walk with Me Sydney' is a novelty song written by Roger Waters, and includes backing vocals from Waters and Juliette Gale. The other three songs were written by Syd Barrett: 'Double O Bo' is an unconvincing Bo Diddley shuffle; 'Remember Me' is a raucous blues shouter and 'Butterfly' has traces of needle surface noise, so presumably this was sourced from an acetate. Some parts of this final song in this batch have distinct hints of Barrett's songs for *The Piper at the Gates of Dawn*: the bridge changes, backing vocals, and a faltering organ solo are precursors to Pink Floyd's future direction.

The Piper at the Gates of Dawn

Recorded February–June 1967 at EMI Studios, Abbey Road, London. Produced by Norman Smith. First released 5 August 1967 (UK: Columbia SX/SXC 6157); 26 October 1967 (US: Tower T/ST 5903).[4]

Pink Floyd's debut album, and their only complete album with Syd Barrett's involvement, was recorded at EMI's studios on Abbey Road, London, concurrently with The Beatles' *Sgt. Pepper's Lonely Hearts Club Band.*

The bulk of *The Piper at the Gates of Dawn* was recorded in two week-long sessions in March and April 1967, with some overdubbing during mixing sessions in June 1967.

> We were finishing songs in one or two days in the studio… the ease of recording was in part due to the fact that we were essentially recording our live set and listening to *Piper* now gives a rough indication of the set list we'd been playing at UFO and the Roundhouse.
>
> Nick Mason in *Inside Out: A Personal History of Pink Floyd (2004)*

Split between the band's concert-improvised lengthy instrumentals ('Astronomy Domine', 'Interstellar Overdrive', and 'Pow R. Toc H.') and Syd Barrett's shorter, more whimsical, songs about scarecrows, bicycles, gnomes, and fairy tales, *The Piper at the Gates of Dawn* is a very much a product of its time. [5]

Special limited editions were issued to mark its 30th and 40th anniversaries in 1997 and 2007.

'Astronomy Domine'[6]

Syd Barrett: lyrics, music, guitars, vocals
Richard Wright: Farfisa organ, vocals
Roger Waters: bass
Nick Mason: drums
Peter Jenner: intro vocalisations

Recorded 11, 12, and 17 April 1967 at EMI Studios, Abbey Road, London.

'Astronomy Domine', the first of Pink Floyd's space-themed songs, opens with the voice of their manager Peter Jenner reading the names of planets through a megaphone. Barrett's crisp guitar and Mason's dynamic drumming dominate: unusual time signatures and a psychedelic jam give this majestic tune the stamp of 1967 authority. The incantatory lyrics mention planets Jupiter, Saturn, and Neptune; as well as Uranian moons Oberon, Miranda, and Titania; and Saturn's moon Titan. It was a popular song live, remaining in the set after Barrett's departure, and was recorded for the live album *Ummagumma* in 1969, as well as being revived during the 1994 tour to promote *The Division Bell.*

The first known performance was in London on 14 October 1966, and it was last performed with Roger Waters in Rome on 20 June 1971. The live version on *Ummagumma* was recorded on 27 April 1969 at the Mothers Club, Birmingham.

Performed regularly by Pink Floyd in 1994, live versions have been released on the *Take It Back* CD single (recorded in Miami, 30 March 1994, released 16 May 1994), and on *P•U•L•S•E* (recorded in London on 15 October 1994, released 29 May 1995). It was also performed by David Gilmour on his solo tours of 2006 and 2015–2016.

'Lucifer Sam'

Syd Barrett: lyrics, music, guitar, vocals
Richard Wright: Farfisa organ, vocals
Roger Waters: bass
Nick Mason: drums, percussion

Recorded 12, 13, 17, and 18 April 1967, 12 and 27 June 1967 at EMI Studios, Abbey Road, London.

Initially recorded with the title 'Percy the Rat Catcher' during sessions in April 1967, a vocal overdub in June 1967, with new lyrics, replaced the previous recordings. It is impossible to believe that unreleased outtakes of this do not exist in EMI's vaults.

First performed in Brighton on 16 April 1967, a few days after being recorded for EMI, 'Lucifer Sam' was performed live by Pink Floyd only in 1967, where it featured as an encore during many performances, mostly notably at the Games for May concert.

'Matilda Mother'

Syd Barrett: lyrics, music, guitars, vocals
Richard Wright: Farfisa organ, Hammond organ, vocals
Roger Waters: bass, vocals
Nick Mason: drums

Recorded 21 February 1967 at EMI Studios, Abbey Road, London.

'Matilda Mother' is 1960s psychedelic London crystallised into three minutes. It is mostly sung by Richard Wright, who also contributes a startling organ solo.

Barrett originally wrote the song around Hilaire Belloc's poem 'Cautionary Tales', but needed to rewrite and rerecord the track when Belloc's estate denied permission to use the lyrics.

> On a Tuesday night, 21 February 1967, Pink Floyd entered EMI Recordings Studios for their first recording session as a professional band. The song they decided to record was Barrett's whimsical song about bad children, 'Matilda's Mother'. Six takes were recorded, with Norman Smith producing. The session was not intended

> to produce a recording for release and was not logged as such. It appears to have been just a test session by EMI to see how the band worked in the studio with their people (EMI insisted on using their own producer and engineers). Two days later, on Thursday, February 23, 1967, Norman Smith and engineer Peter Mew did a rough mix of take 6 of 'Matilda's Mother,' presumably as a demo for EMI management to hear. It must have made an impression, as five days later, on 28 February 1967, EMI signed the group to a recording contract (which covered their recordings beginning on 20 February 1967—thus including the recording of 'Matilda's Mother' from the 21st). Here began the professional recording career of Pink Floyd.
>
> Vernon Fitch, *Hey You*, issue #11 (December 2007)

One assumes that this is the version released in 2007 on the 40th anniversary edition of *The Piper at the Gates of Dawn*; it has some different verse lyrics and extra guitar. This same version, duly remixed, was released again on both *An Introduction to Syd Barrett* (2010) and *The Early Years 1965–1972* (2016). The most recent version fades much later, threatening to segue into a typical 1967 Pink Floyd jam.

The first known performance of 'Matilda Mother' was in London on 14 October 1966, and the song was performed regularly until June 1968. It was recorded at a session for BBC Radio on 25 September 1967 and released on *The Early Years 1965–1972* box set in 2016. A full-bodied live version recorded in Stockholm on 10 December 1967 (with an almost inaudible Barrett vocal and a very hit-and-miss bass performance from Roger Waters) was released on *The Early Years 1965–1972* in 2016.

'Flaming'

Syd Barrett: lyrics, music, guitars, vocals
Richard Wright: Farfisa organ, Hammond organ, Lowrey organ, piano, vocals
Roger Waters: bass, slide whistle, vocals
Nick Mason: drums, percussion

Recorded 16 March 1967 at EMI Studios, Abbey Road, London.

'Flaming' is a more-or-less straight pop/rock song, but one with a complex, swirling arrangement which lifts it above many of the other songs on *The Piper at the Gates of Dawn*.

Not included on the US release of *The Piper at the Gates of Dawn*, 'Flaming' was issued as a single in the US in November 1967 in an alternative—and quite different—mono mix. This mix was later used on the US edition of *A Nice Pair* and is only available from these two sources. The B-side of this release was 'The Gnome'.

The first known performance of 'Flaming' was at the Games for May concert in London on 12 May 1967. It was recorded at a session for BBC Radio on 25 September 1967 and released on *The Early Years 1965–1972* box set in 2016; sung by David Gilmour after Barrett's departure, the song remained in the band's repertoire until the end of 1968, including a live recording for the French TV show *Tous en Scène*.

'Pow R. Toc H.'

Syd Barrett: music, guitars, vocals
Richard Wright: music, Farfisa organ, piano, vocals
Roger Waters: music, bass, vocals
Nick Mason: music, drums, percussion

Recorded 21 March 1967 at EMI Studios, Abbey Road, London.

A strident free-form jam, written collectively by the band, mostly on one note. This might have sounded great in the UFO Club in 1967, but the studio cut does not merit more than one listen today. Later live versions were much better, with real dynamism—imagine an up-tempo arrangement of 'Careful with That Axe, Eugene'.

The recording of 'Pow R. Toc H.' on 21 March 1967 was the day that Pink Floyd met The Beatles, who were working on 'Lovely Rita' and 'Good Morning, Good Morning' at EMI that day.

> The encounter was cautious—a shame in that, at this stage, the Floyd's music more closely resembled The Beatles' than any other group in the country. John Lennon and Syd Barrett had much in common as songwriters, but it was Paul McCartney who had heard the Floyd at UFO and complimented them on the musical direction they were taking.
>
> Ian MacDonald, *Revolution in the Head* (1994)

> We were ushered into Studio 2. The music sounded wonderful and incredibly, professional. We sat at the back of the control room and after a suitable (and embarrassing) period of time had elapsed we were ushered out.
>
> Nick Mason in *Inside Out: A Personal History of Pink Floyd* (2004)

The first known performance was in London on 14 October 1966 and it was retained until mid-1968, and then was brought back to the set in 1969 as part of *The Man and the Journey*. Three versions of this song were released on *The Early Years 1965–1972* in 2016: a live version recorded in Stockholm on 10 December 1967; a session for BBC Radio on 20 December 1967; and a recording for Dutch radio on 17 September 1969.

'Take Up Thy Stethoscope and Walk'

Syd Barrett: guitars, vocals
Richard Wright: Farfisa organ, piano and vocals
Roger Waters: lyrics, music, bass, vocals
Nick Mason: drums, timpani

Recorded 20 March 1967 at EMI Studios, Abbey Road, London.

This is Roger Waters' songwriting debut: a difficult, clinical, morbid, discordant song with a lyrical theme that harks forward twelve years to 'Comfortably Numb'. The title comes from the Bible passage John 5:8—'Jesus saith unto him, Rise, take up thy bed, and walk'.

First performed in London on 14 October 1966, this song would not survive the Barrett-era.

'Interstellar Overdrive'

Syd Barrett: music, guitars
Richard Wright: music, organ
Roger Waters: music, bass
Nick Mason: music, drums
Norman Smith: drum roll

Recorded 16 March, 5 June, and 27 June 1967 at EMI Studios, Abbey Road, London.

Listening to the stereo mix of 'Interstellar Overdrive' on headphones today is still a brain-bending experience. The song origins lie in the tune 'My Little Red Book', which had been written by Burt Bacharach and Hal David for the film *What's New Pussycat* (1965) and recorded by Manfred Mann. A heavier arrangement was a minor US hit for Love in March 1966. As the story goes, Syd Barrett heard Peter Jenner humming 'My Little Red Book' and Barrett tried to play the melody on his guitar. Roger Waters, for his part, suggests that 'Interstellar Overdrive' is a variation on the theme tune to the UK TV series *Steptoe and Son* (1962–1974).

Whatever the story, 'Interstellar Overdrive' is probably the most important song on *The Piper at the Gates of Dawn* in terms of Pink Floyd's immediate post-Barrett direction, as their songs then started to extend in length and complexity, with carefully composed structures and themes.

> 'Interstellar Overdrive' formed a central plank of our live shows. Based around Syd's riff, the piece would generally be played with different elements structured in the same order each time.
>
> Nick Mason in *Inside Out: A Personal History of Pink Floyd* (2004)

'Interstellar Overdrive' was recorded a number of times before the band signed for EMI. It was first recorded as a demo on 31 October 1966 for the film *San Francisco*.[7] A longer recording of 'Interstellar Overdrive' can be heard on the soundtrack to the film *Tonite Let's All Make Love in London*; this was recorded at Sound Technique Studios, London on 11 January 1967. Two alternative EMI versions were included on the 40th anniversary edition of *The Piper at the Gates of Dawn*: Take 2 (27 February 1967), released on an EP in France; and the shorter Take 6 (16 March 1967).

The song was placed last on the US 1967 release of *The Piper at the Gates of Dawn* album and subsequently fades a few seconds early to remove the segue into 'The Gnome'. The version on *Relics* uses the original master tape and removes the segue without fading, thus bringing the song to a natural ending.

One of Pink Floyd's first compositions, dating from the early months of 1966, 'Interstellar Overdrive' was performed live through to the end of 1971, often as an encore. Three live versions of 'Interstellar Overdrive' were released on *The Early Years 1965–1972* in 2016: a live recording from Stockholm (10 December 1967), a performance recorded for BBC radio (20 December 1968) and a very slow mixed-to-stereo live rendition from Amsterdam (9 August 1969)—but yet, the astonishing outtake from the *Ummagumma* recording sessions remains unreleased.

'Interstellar Overdrive' was one of a number of songs on the short-list for inclusion on the 2001 best-of *Echoes* but ultimately rejected.[8]

'The Gnome'

Syd Barrett: lyrics, music, guitars, vocals
Richard Wright: celesta, vibraphone
Roger Waters: bass, vocals
Nick Mason: percussion

Recorded 20 March 1967 at EMI Studios, Abbey Road, London.

The final four songs on *The Piper at the Gates of Dawn* are lesser examples of psychedelic pop and their worth in the overall Pink Floyd canon is slight. 'The Gnome', released as the B-side of 'Flaming' in the US on 2 November 1967, tells the story of scarlet-tunic-wearing Grimble Gromble.[9]

Recorded for the BBC on 25 September 1967 and released on *The Early Years 1965–1972* box set in 2016. It was performed live from October 1966–September 1967.

'Chapter 24'

Syd Barrett: lyrics, music, guitars, vocals
Richard Wright: Farfisa organ, Hohner Pianet, cello, harmonium, vocals
Roger Waters: bass, gong
Nick Mason: percussion

Recorded 27 February and 15 March 1967 at EMI Studios, Abbey Road, London.

The lyrics from 'Chapter 24' are quoted almost verbatim from the ancient Chinese tome *I Ching*. The song is known to have been performed only once, 19 May 1967 at Club-a-Go-Go in Newcastle-upon-Tyne, but was likely performed at other dates in this period.

'The Scarecrow'

Syd Barrett: lyrics, music, guitars, vocals
Richard Wright: Farfisa organ, flute, cello, vocals
Roger Waters: bass, slide whistle, vocals
Nick Mason: drums, percussion

Recorded 22 March 1967 at EMI Studios, Abbey Road, London.

'The Scarecrow': in which Syd Barrett compares his own existence to that of a scarecrow. A psychedelic/folk hybrid arrangement hides an early hint of a perennial Pink Floyd theme—fate.

> The black and green scarecrow is sadder than me / But now he's resigned to his fate / 'Cause life's not unkind—he doesn't mind.

This theme— that we should be in charge of our own destiny—would recur again in their later work; songs such as 'Time' and 'One Slip' would also explore this subject.

The inclusion of 12-string guitar and a cello extend the musical palette of a band that was well-served by their producer Norman Smith. Smith provided musical colour to these early recordings by encouraging the band to move outside their guitar/bass/drums/organ format.

'The Scarecrow' was performed a handful of times in autumn 1967, recorded at a session for BBC Radio on 25 September 1967, and released on *The Early Years 1965–1972* box set in 2016.

'Bike'

Syd Barrett: lyrics, music, guitars, vocals
Richard Wright: harmonium, violin, celesta, piano, vocals
Roger Waters: bass, vocals
Nick Mason: drums, percussion

Recorded 21 May and 5 June 1967 at EMI Studios, Abbey Road, London.

A song in which our Syd impresses a presumed love interest with a bicycle, a cloak, a mouse, and some gingerbread men.

The final section is a remarkable example of *music concrete*—a studio-constructed collage of bells, clocks, gongs, and other sounds. If The Beatles' 'Revolution #9' is the most widely-heard example of avant-garde music ever recorded, then 'Bike' must be a close second.

'Bike' was not included on the US release of *The Piper at the Gates of Dawn*, and instead received its first US release on *Relics* (15 July 1971).

No known live performances.

Reviews

> The psychedelic image of the group really comes to life on this LP, which is a fine showcase for both their talent and the recording technique. Plenty of mind-blowing sound.
>
> Record Mirror

> *The Piper at the Gates of Dawn* successfully captures both sides of psychedelic experimentation—the pleasures of expanding one's mind and perception and an underlying threat of mental disorder and even lunacy; this duality makes Piper all the more compelling in light of Barrett's subsequent breakdown and ranks it as one of the best psychedelic albums of all time.
>
> Steve Huey, AllMusic

> Filled with the child-poet musings of a mind not yet oppressed, but free to wander between fairy tales and cosmic explorations and still be home in time for tea.
>
> Chris Jones, BBC (2007)

> I thought it was fuckin' awful.
>
> Pete Townshend

A Saucerful of Secrets (1968)

Recorded August 1967–May 1968, EMI Studios, Abbey Road, London and De Lane Lea Studios, Kingsway, London. Produced by Norman Smith. First released 29 June 1968 (UK: Columbia SX/XCS 6258); 27 July 1968 (US: Tower T/ST 5131)

A Saucerful of Secrets is a schizophrenic album, recorded over a period of several months either side of Syd Barrett's departure. Two tracks were recorded for a possible single in August 1967, followed by four sessions in October–November 1967, one in December 1967, and sporadic recording in January, February, and April 1968.

In addition to 'Jugband Blues', the album was originally to include the Barrett compositions 'Vegetable Man' and 'Scream Thy Last Scream'.

'Let There Be More Light'

Richard Wright: Farfisa and Hammond organ, vocals, piano
David Gilmour: guitars, vocals
Roger Waters: lyrics, music, bass, vocals
Nick Mason: drums, percussion

Recorded 18 January 1968 at EMI Studios, Abbey Road, London and released as a single in the US (19 August 1968).

The first song recorded for *A Saucerful of Secrets* without Syd Barrett, 'Let There Be More Light' is a sometimes frantic, sometimes broody Waters sci-fi song. Extending on a one-chord jam well beyond its best before date, suitably edited, 'Let There Be More Light' would be Pink Floyd's fourth American single.

It was first performed for French TV at ORTF TV Studios, Buttes Chaumont, Paris, on 21 February 1968, and was included in the band's set list until the end of 1969. The song was recorded 'live in the studio' for BBC Radio on 25 June 1968, and released on *The Early Years 1965–1972* box set in 2016; it was also recorded for Dutch radio on 17 September 1969, and released on *The Early Years 1965–1972*.

'Remember a Day'

Richard Wright: lyrics, music, Farfisa organ, piano, vocals
Roger Waters: bass
Syd Barrett: guitars, vocals
Norman Smith: drums, backing vocals

Recorded 9–12 October 1967 at De Lane Lea Studios, Kingsway, London, and released as the B-side to 'Let There Be More Light' in the US (19 August 1968).

This Richard Wright song includes a slide guitar solo by Syd Barrett—sweetened here and there, some sources suggest, by David Gilmour during later sessions—and drums by producer Norman Smith who took over at the kit when Nick Mason couldn't get the feel that Smith wanted.

> [I] did play on another track written by Richard Wright. I forget the title but it had a steel guitar in the background.

Syd Barrett, quoted in *Syd Barrett & Pink Floyd: Dark Globe* by Julian Palacios (2010)

> 'Remember a Day' is inoffensive, but features some rather miserable bottleneck guitar, second rate piano and empty-sounding acoustic guitar work.
>
> Jim Miller, *Rolling Stone* (October 1968)

It was performed only twice, both times as an encore in May 1968. David Gilmour performed the song on a live broadcast of *Later... with Jools Holland* on 23 September 2008 as a tribute to Richard Wright, who had died eight days earlier.

'Set the Controls for the Heart of the Sun'

Richard Wright: Farfisa organ, celesta, vibraphone
David Gilmour: guitar
Roger Waters: lyrics, music, bass, vocals, gong
Syd Barrett: guitar
Nick Mason: drums

Recorded 7–8 August 1967, 23 October 1967, and 11 January 1968 at EMI Studios, Abbey Road, London.

The strongest song on the album, the almost lethargic 'Set the Controls for the Heart of the Sun'—with a detached, half-whispered vocal by Waters and insistent, metronomic drums from Nick Mason—displays a clear post-Barrett development, despite being recorded with Barrett during the first sessions for the album. Later overdubs added David Gilmour's guitar to the mix, this song thus becoming the only Pink Floyd song to feature both Barrett and Gilmour. The lyrics are borrowed from Chinese poetry, most notably from *Poems of the late T'ang* by A.C. Graham and a 1965 book by Michael Moorcock entitled *The Fireclown*.

'Set the Controls for the Heart of the Sun' was introduced to Pink Floyd's live set at the end of April 1967. It was regularly performed for the next six and a half years—including at least six times with both Barrett and Gilmour together in the group—through to the autumn of 1973.

Several live versions have been released:

Recorded for BBC Radio on 25 September 1967, released on *The Early Years 1965–1972*
Recorded in Stockholm on 10 December 1967, released on *The Early Years 1965–1972*
Recorded for *Ummagumma* on 2 May 1969 at Manchester College of Commerce
Recorded in Amsterdam on 9 August 1969 in stereo, but with almost inaudible vocals, released on *The Early Years 1965–1972*
Recorded at Brighton Dome, 29 June 1972, available on the Immersion box set of *The Dark Side of the Moon* released in 2011
Recorded 'live-in-the-studio' version for *Live in Pompeii* in Studio Europasonor, Paris, from 13–20 December 1972. This, too, was released on *The Early Years 1965–1972*

'Corporal Clegg'

Richard Wright: Farfisa organ, vocals
David Gilmour: guitars, vocals, kazoo
Roger Waters: lyrics, music, bass, vocals
Nick Mason: drums, percussion, vocals

Recorded 24 January 1968 at EMI Studios, Abbey Road, London.

Waters' oblique and dark rumination on the loss of his father in the Second World War, the heavily ironic lyrics of 'Corporal Clegg' have stayed relevant, while the music arrangement is firmly 1968. The lyrical theme would be revisited again in the coming years, particularly in *The Wall* and throughout *The Final Cut*.

The song is known to only have been performed a few times, including for German TV on 22 July 1969. Considering the subject matter—the loss of his father in the Second World War—one assumes that this was a ghoulish joke on the part of Roger Waters.

'A Saucerful of Secrets'

Richard Wright: music, Farfisa and Hammond organ, vocals, piano, mellotron, vibraphone
David Gilmour: music, guitars, vocals
Roger Waters: music, bass, cymbals
Nick Mason: music, drums, percussion

Recorded April 1968 at EMI Studios, Abbey Road, London.

In the final three minutes of 'A Saucerful of Secrets', we hear the birth of progressive rock.

> With the track 'A Saucerful of Secrets' it started becoming more clear to me where we were going.
>
> David Gilmour, interviewed for *The Pink Floyd and Syd Barrett Story* television documentary (2001)

'A Saucerful of Secrets' patches together four disparate segments, the genesis of a new method of composing that would be refined through the next several albums:

The tension of 'Something Else' (0:00–3:57) comprising cymbals, organ, and slide guitar;
The aggression of the experimental free-form almost jazz improvisation of 'Syncopated Pandemonium' (3:57–7:04) made up of drum tape loop, cymbals, distorted guitars and piano;
The slow, transitional 'Storm Signal' (7:04–8:38), chimes and organ;
The organ-led requiem 'Celestial Voices' (8:38–11:52) recorded with bass, organ, mellotron and chorus.

> 'A Saucerful of Secrets' was one of those where we went into the studio with no pre-conceived ideas.
>
> Richard Wright, *New Musical Express* (27 May 1972)

> The architecture students [drew] these peaks and troughs on a chart, working out where the piece was going to go.
>
> David Gilmour, *Musician* (1982)

'Celestial Voices', especially in concert where the bass and drums would be much more prominent, is a strong contender for the first true progressive rock song. Here, at last, was a way forward, and not just for Pink Floyd. Almost all of the genre's major bands, including Jethro Tull, King Crimson, Yes, Genesis, Van der Graaf Generator, ELP, Gentle Giant, and Curved Air, released their debut albums during the years 1968–1970, in the wake of *A Saucerful of Secrets*.

> The album's title track is eleven minutes of psychedelic muzak, hardly electronic music, but hardly creative rock either. There's a lot of interesting noise and at times one almost is tempted to take the whole conglomeration as a significant experimental probe. But as the chaos settles reassuringly into a banal organ-cum-religious chorus final, one realizes that the Pink Floyd are firmly anchored in the diatonic world with any deviations from that norm a matter of effect rather than musical conviction.
>
> Jim Miller, *Rolling Stone* (October 1968)

> The use of electronic effects on 'A Saucerful of Secrets' is poorly handled and does not add up to music. It is too long, too boring and totally uninventive, particularly when compared to a similar electronic composition such as 'Metamorphosis' by Vladimir Ussachevsky, which was done in 1957, eleven years ago.
>
> Miles, *International Times* (26 July 1968)

The first known performance of 'A Saucerful of Secrets' is from the Paradiso, Amsterdam on 23 May 1968, and the last at Winterland, San Francisco on 24 November 1972.

There are several live versions available:

A session recorded 'live in the studio' for BBC Radio on 25 June 1968 and released on *The Early Years 1965–1972* box set in 2016.[10]

The live version on *Ummagumma* was recorded on 27 April 1969 at the Mothers Club, Birmingham.

An in-concert recording from Amsterdam, 9 August 1969 was released on *The Early Years 1965–1972*.

'Syncopated Pandemonium' was one of the many tracks played as 'Doing It' in the conceptual concert suite *The Man and the Journey* during 1969, and the 'Celestial Voices' section was used as the finale to this same concept, renamed 'The End of the Beginning'. Versions of both of these were recorded for Dutch radio on 17 September 1969 and released on *The Early Years 1965–1972*.

A terrific live-without-an-audience version was recorded in Pompeii for *Live in Pompeii* between 4 and 7 October 1971. This was released on *The Early Years 1965–1972*.

'See-Saw'

Richard Wright: lyrics, music, vocals, piano, Farfisa organ, xylophone, mellotron
David Gilmour: guitars, vocals
Roger Waters: bass
Nick Mason: drums, percussion
Norman Smith: backing vocals

Recorded 24 January 1968 at EMI Studios, Abbey Road, London.

Written solely by Richard Wright, and mostly sung by him, the lyrics are vague enough to suggest a troubled brother-sister relationship, or perhaps a reflection on Syd Barrett and one of his girlfriends. Some tempo and key changes barely hold the interest of the listener.

The band's wry working title 'The Most Boring Song I've Ever Heard Bar Two' is not so far off the mark.

> Richard Wright: ['See Saw' and 'Remember a Day'] are a sort of an embarrassment. I don't think I've listened to them ever since we recorded them. It was a learning process. Through writing these songs, I learned that I'm not a lyric writer, for example. But you have to try it before you find out. The lyrics are appalling—terrible—but so were a lot of lyrics in those days.[11]

No known live performances.

'Jugband Blues'

Syd Barrett: lyrics, music, guitars, vocals
Richard Wright: keyboards, tin whistle
Roger Waters: bass
Nick Mason: drums, percussion and kazoo
The Salvation Army Band

Recorded 19 October 1967 at De Lane Lea Studios, Kingsway, London.

This was Syd Barrett's utterly heartbreaking final contribution to Pink Floyd. Although this song was recorded three months before Barrett's departure from the band, Syd, even in his then-troubled state, must have realised that the game was almost up.

> It's awfully considerate of you to think of me here / And I'm much obliged to you for making it clear that I'm not here.

> 'Syd knew exactly what was happening to him, but he was powerless to stop it. He knew he was going wrong inside.'
>
> Andrew King, Pink Floyd manager (1966-1968)

With its downbeat final lyrics, placing the disjointed 'Jugband Blues' at the end of *A Saucerful of Secrets* closed the lid on the Syd Barrett era once and for all.

> It is almost a poetic recitation by Barrett, with avant-garde sound effects by the group. The centre passage is almost free form pop, with six members of the Salvation Army on the recording session told to 'play what you like.'
>
> *Melody Maker* (9 December 1967)

> An extraordinary song, the ultimate self-diagnosis on a state of schizophrenia. Powerful disturbing art.
>
> Peter Jenner, Pink Floyd manager (1966–1968)

The song was remixed with more echo, phasing, and stereo panning for *An Introduction to Syd Barrett* in 2010. This superior mix was also included on *The Early Years* box set that was released in 2016.

'Jugband Blues' is known to be have been performed only once, for BBC Radio at Maida Vale Studio 4, London on 20 December 1967. This was released on *The Early Years 1965–1972.*

Reviews

> With Barrett gone we are left with the work of bassist Roger Waters and organist Rick Wright. Waters (who wrote a couple of dull tracks on the first album) is an uninteresting writer, vocalist and bass player. The production work is not as glittery as the first album's and the instrumental work is shoddy and routine.
>
> Jim Miller, Rolling Stone (October 1968)

Related Singles and Other Contemporary Songs 1967–1968

'Scream Thy Last Scream'

Syd Barrett: lyrics, music, guitars, vocals
Roger Waters: bass
Richard Wright: keyboards
Nick Mason: drums, vocals

Recorded 7–8 August 1967 at De Lane Lea Studios, Kingsway, London and EMI Studios, Abbey Road, London.

Recorded as a possible follow up to 'See Emily Play' in August 1967, 'Scream Thy Last Scream' is a difficult listen. The track's B-side was initially planned to be 'Set the Controls for the Heart of the Sun' and later 'Vegetable Man', but the single was ultimately cancelled and this song remained unreleased for nearly fifty years. High quality stereo versions were commonly available in collectors' circles for years until the song was finally released as part of the immense *The Early Years 1965–1972* box set in November 2016. The song's chord progression and melody were later reworked for Barrett's song 'Baby Lemonade'.

'Scream Thy Last Scream' was performed live a number of times between September and December 1967. A live version with inaudible vocals, recorded in Stockholm (10 December 1967), and a studio session for BBC Radio (20 December 1967) were both released on *The Early Years 1965–1972* box set.

'Sunshine'

Written by Syd Barrett.

An incomplete backing track recorded at Sound Techniques on 4 September 1967. The song is instrumental and the first 90 seconds of the recording are available on various bootlegs.

'Reaction in G'

This song was performed as a cynical response to audiences and promoters pressuring Pink Floyd to play 'Arnold Layne' and 'See Emily Play'. It was first recorded at a session for BBC Radio on 25 September 1967 and later recorded live in Stockholm on 10 December 1967 as a superb slice of coherent, driving, psychedelic rock. Both versions can be heard on *The Early Years 1965-1972.*

'Vegetable Man'

Syd Barrett: lyrics, music, guitars, vocals
Richard Wright: keyboards, vocals
Roger Waters: bass, vocals
Nick Mason: drums, percussion, vocals

Recorded 9–12 October 1967 at De Lane Lea Studios, Kingsway, London.

A churning, almost tuneless song recorded in October 1967. High quality stereo versions were commonly available in collectors' circles for years until the song was finally released as part of *The Early Years 1965–1972* box set in November 2016. It is a discordant mess, and only the enduring legend of Syd Barrett has driven any interest in this raucous and pointless outtake.

> It was really stressful waiting for Syd to come up with the songs for the second album. Everybody was looking at him and he couldn't do it. The last Floyd song Syd wrote, 'Vegetable Man', was done for those sessions, though it never came out. He wrote it round at my house; it's just a description of what he's wearing. It's very disturbing. Roger took it off the album because it was too dark and it is. It's like psychological flashing.
>
> Peter Jenner, Pink Floyd manager (1966–1968), interviewed in *Mojo*, 1994

Known to be have been performed only once, for BBC radio on 20 December 1967, this BBC version was released on *The Early Years 1965–1972* box set in 2016.

'In the Beechwoods'

Written by Syd Barrett.

An unreleased song from the sessions for *A Saucerful of Secrets* at De Lane Lea in October 1967: the same sessions that yielded 'Jugband Blues', 'Remember a Day' and 'Vegetable Man'. It is a lovely, if incomplete, instrumental backing track, strong in its own right, initially driven by drums and keyboards, and featuring a central section with a furious R&B rave-up—an enjoyable period piece

Released (in a '2010 remix') on *The Early Years 1965–1972*.

'Apples and Oranges'

Syd Barrett: lyrics, music, guitar, vocals
Richard Wright: Hammond organ, piano, electric piano, vocals
Roger Waters: bass, vocals
Nick Mason: drums, tambourine

Recorded 26–27 October 1967 at De Lane Lea Studios, Kingsway, London.

Released as a single on 18 November 1967. Pink Floyd's follow-up to 'See Emily Play', this is early-Floyd-by-numbers. It is the story of a shopping trip: it is a resounding miss.

> It's unlike anything we've ever done before. It's a new sound. Got a lot of guitar in it. It's a happy song and it's got a touch of Christmas. It's about a girl who I saw just walking round town, in Richmond.
>
> Syd Barrett quoted in *Top Pops and Music Now* (1967)

> We all thought it was a really good song, but the recording didn't come up so well.
>
> Richard Wright, *New Musical Express* (27 May 1972)

> 'Apples and Oranges' was destroyed by the production. It's a fucking good song.
>
> Roger Waters quoted in *Saucerful of Secrets: The Pink Floyd Odyssey* (Nicholas Schaffner, 1991)

The only known live performance of 'Apples and Oranges' was for the BBC on 25 September 1967. This seemingly was not broadcast with the rest of the set the following week, and does not appear on *The Early Years 1965–1972*, despite the existence of a reasonable quality recording.

'John Latham'

Nine (yes, nine) previously unheard stereo studio outtakes of this long-rumoured song, recorded in October 1967, were released in 2016 on *The Early Years 1965–1972*. Nothing more than extended extrapolations of the central section of 'Interstellar Overdrive' these nine versions have been mixed into a single joyful listening experience, comprising thirty minutes of discordant, unstructured racket. Presumably these pieces were recorded for, or in honour of, the London-based performance artist John Latham (1921–2004) who was active in counter-culture art during this period.

'Paint Box'

Richard Wright: lyrics, music, vocals, piano
Syd Barrett: guitars, vocals
Roger Waters: bass, vocals
Nick Mason: drums

Recorded 1 November 1967 at De Lane Lea Studios, Kingsway, London and released as the B-side to 'Apples and Oranges' on 18 November 1967.

Recorded a few days after 'Apples and Oranges', specifically as the B-side to that song, this is surely the better track. Familiar to millions as the fifth track on the *Relics* compilation (released in 1971), 'Paint Box' was Richard Wright's first solo writing credit, and is the band's first comment on the vagaries of fame. No known live performances.

> I didn't think Paint Box would make a great single, actually. I know it wouldn't, in fact.
>
> Richard Wright, New Musical Express (27 May 1972)

'It Would Be So Nice'

Richard Wright: lyrics, music, vocals, piano, mellotron, Farfisa organ, recorder
David Gilmour: guitars, vocals
Roger Waters: bass, vocals
Nick Mason: drums

Recorded 12–13 January 1968 at EMI Studios, Abbey Road, London and released as a single on 12 April 1968.

Recorded as the first post-Barrett single, and not so far from the music of The Kinks and The Monkees, this mundane song, an account of a dull day, was another unquestionable miss. Due to mentioning the daily newspaper *The Evening Standard* in the original lyrics, the band was forced to return in the studio to change the words to reference the fictional Daily Standard instead. The original *Evening Standard* version does not seem to have surfaced. The only known live performance of 'It Would Be So Nice' was in Brighton on 11 May 1968.

> The first recorded work released in the wake of Syd Barrett's exit was [the] almost unbearably whimsical 'It Would Be So Nice', a single whose lightweight strain of pop-psychedelia rendered it a non-event that failed to trouble the British charts.
>
> John Harris, *The Dark Side of the Moon: The Making of Pink Floyd's Masterpiece* (2005)

> At that period we had no direction. We were being hustled about [making] hit singles. There's so many people saying it's important [that] you start to think it is important.
>
> Nick Mason, *Disk* (23 August 1975)

'Julia Dream'

Richard Wright: mellotron, Hammond organ, vocals
David Gilmour: guitars, vocals
Roger Waters: lyrics, music, bass, vocals
Nick Mason: percussion

Recorded 12–13 January 1968 at EMI Studios, Abbey Road, London and released as a single on 12 April 1968.

The B-side of 'It Would Be So Nice', this was the first released Pink Floyd song that was sung by David Gilmour. Pleasant enough, but with Waters' typically dark imagery, 'Julia Dream' was a forebear to the acoustic side of Pink Floyd that would temper their cosmic indulgences in years to come.

'Julia Dream' was recorded for the BBC at 201 Piccadilly Studios, London on 25 June 1968; this performance was released on *The Early Years 1965–1972* box set in 2016. No other performances are known.

'Song 1' / 'Roger's Boogie'

Two previously unknown and unheard songs recorded at Capitol Studios, Los Angeles on 22 August 1968 and released on *The Early Years 1965–1972* box set in November 2016. 'Song 1' is tentative and very clearly incomplete, but, with some unusual time changes and parts reminiscent of 'Cymbaline', it is a shame it was not developed further.

Meanwhile, 'Roger's Boogie'—an ironic title—sounds like nothing else in the Pink Floyd catalogue. This astonishing piece, with chanting backing vocals, irregular tempo, descending guitar patterns, and shifting chord changes, is straight from the Radiohead song book. What a find!

'Music from The Committee No. 1' / 'Music from The Committee No. 2'

Two short excerpts, out of nine available, for Pink Floyd's soundtrack to the 1968 film *The Committee*, both seemingly extracted directly from the film itself. No. 1 is a short, up-tempo sequence of chords from the full band; No. 2 is a rewrite of the final section of 'A Saucerful of Secrets'. Both were released on 2016's *The Early Years 1965–1972* box set.

'Point Me at the Sky'

David Gilmour: lyrics, music, guitars, vocals
Roger Waters: lyrics, music, bass, vocals
Richard Wright: Hammond organ, piano, glockenspiel, vocals
Nick Mason: drums, percussion

Recorded 3 November 1968 at EMI Studios, Abbey Road, London and released as a single on 17 December 1968 (UK: Columbia DB 8511).

Pink Floyd's final attempt at a single in the 1960s. This early Waters / Gilmour collaboration was released in mid-December 1968, and, as with 'Apples and Oranges' and 'It Would Be So Nice', did not trouble the chart compilers. The uplifting effect of its lightweight verses, with hints of progressive rock in their execution, is destroyed by the concrete blocks of the unsubtle chorus.

Pointedly ignored by every Pink Floyd compilation from *Relics* onwards, 'Point Me at the Sky' was finally released digitally on CD and as a download in 2016: 48 years and 1 week after its initial release. It was performed for the BBC on 20 December 1968, and released, as with the single cut, on *The Early Years 1965–1972* box set. No other performances are known.

'Careful with That Axe, Eugene'

Roger Waters: music, bass, vocals
David Gilmour: music, guitar, vocals
Richard Wright: music, Hammond organ, vibraphone
Nick Mason: music, drums

Recorded 4 November 1968 at EMI Studios, Abbey Road, London and released on 17 December 1968 as the B-side to 'Point Me at the Sky' (UK: Columbia DB 8511).

An unusual choice for a B-side perhaps, but part of the Pink Floyd legend due to its inclusion on the *Relics* compilation album and the enduring live renditions on *Ummagumma* and *Live in Pompeii*. 'Careful with That Axe, Eugene' is a superb exercise in dynamics and the release of pent-up aggression. It plays out its almost six-minute length on a single chord, and yet remains entertaining, engaging, and exciting throughout. One of the very best early Pink Floyd songs, it was rerecorded —and, indeed, improved—as 'Come in No. 51 Your Time Is Up' on the soundtrack to *Zabriskie Point*.

The first known performance of 'Careful with That Axe, Eugene' (at that time called 'Keep Smiling People') was at the Paradiso, Amsterdam on 23 May 1968. It was also included in *The Man and the Journey* suite as 'Beset by Creatures of the Deep'. A regular in the set through to 1973, 'Careful with That Axe, Eugene' was performed for the last time as a surprise encore at the Oakland Coliseum on 9 May 1977.

Nine live versions of 'Careful with That Axe, Eugene' have been released:

Recorded 'live in the studio' for BBC radio on 25 June 1968 (titled 'Murderotic Woman' at this point) and released on *The Early Years 1965–1972* box set in 2016

Recorded on 2 May 1969 at Manchester College of Commerce and released on *Ummagumma* later that year.

A live-in-the-studio version for BBC radio was recorded on 12 May 1969 and released on *The Early Years 1965–1972* box set in 2016.

An in-concert recording from Amsterdam, 9 August 1969 was released on *The Early Years 1965–1972.*

Recorded for Dutch radio on 17 September 1969 and released on *The Early Years 1965–1972.*

Recorded for BBC radio on 16 July 1970, released on *The Early Years 1965–1972.*

Two versions recorded for *Live at Pompeii* in Studio Europasonor, Paris, from 13–20 December 1971, released on *The Early Years 1965–1972.*

Recorded at Brighton Dome, 29 June 1972, and available on the Immersion box set of *The Dark Side of the Moon* released in 2011.

2

Floyd Phase 2: 1969–1970 Filling in Time

More (1969)

Recorded February–May 1969, Pye Studios, London, and produced by Pink Floyd. First released 13 June 1969 (UK: Columbia SCX 6346); 9 August 1969 (US: Tower ST 5169)

More was a Top 10 album in the UK, despite only having four songs of note. It was recorded as a soundtrack to the film of the same name, directed by Iranian-born Barbet Schroeder.

> I went to London and took a print of the film *More* and showed it to them. I didn't want typical film music. I wanted this to be the music that the characters were listening to.
>
> Barbet Schroeder quoted in *Pigs Might Fly: The Inside Story of Pink Floyd* (Mark Blake, 2007)

> We have to do it in a week, which is very cool because otherwise we'd spend three months doing it, going back and changing all the time.
>
> Nick Mason, quoted in *Disc and Music Echo* (February 1969)

At a time when Pink Floyd's reputation was being built on their live shows—over fifty concerts in the second half of 1968, almost eighty more in 1969—their recorded output in 1969 was patchy at best.

Of the thirteen pieces included on this album, only four bear repeated listening. Two of these ('Cirrus Minor' and 'The Nile Song') were included on the *Relics* compilation album in 1971, while the two others were part of the band's live set between 1969 and 1971 ('Green Is the Colour' and 'Cymbaline').

Pink Floyd would work again for Schroeder on his film *La Vallée* in 1972.

'Cirrus Minor'

David Gilmour: guitar, vocals
Richard Wright: Hammond organ, Farfisa organ
Roger Waters: lyrics, music

A bucolic, acoustic song with a double-tracked Gilmour vocal and a drawn-out organ finale copped from 'A Saucerful of Secrets'.

The stately coda combines rumbling Hammond and swirling, echo-laden Farfisa, and is an admirable example of the texture that Richard Wright's instrumentation brought to the early recordings of Pink Floyd.

No known live performances.

'The Nile Song'

David Gilmour: guitars, vocals
Roger Waters: lyrics, music, bass
Nick Mason: drums

Released as a single in 1969 in France, Japan, and New Zealand.

Gilmour lets loose on this loud rocker—the wildest (and probably most straightforward) song in the Pink Floyd canon. This being Pink Floyd, the power-trio arrangement hides a complex musical structure where each verse starts in a different key, rising through a several modulations.

The lyrics also use the phrase 'she is bound to drag me down', imagery which was reused years later to great effect in 'Dogs'.

No known live performances.

'Crying Song'

David Gilmour: guitars, vocals
Richard Wright: vibraphone
Nick Mason: snare drum
Roger Waters: lyrics, music, bass

A second pensive and folky acoustic song, comprising of vocals, acoustic guitar, slide guitar, bass, snare drum and vibraphone. Gilmour plays slide guitar, an early example of a style and tone he would make his own in years to come.

No known live performances.

'Up the Khyber'

Richard Wright: music, organ, piano
Nick Mason: music, drums, percussion
Roger Waters: bass

A unique song in the Pink Floyd canon: it is the only one with a Wright/Mason writing credit, and there are layers of studio echo and hints of Wright's love for free-form modern jazz. This piece was sometimes performed as the 'Doing It' section of *The Man and the Journey* suite in 1969. The title is a play on words in the risqué Carry On tradition—*Carry on Up the Khyber* had been released in September 1968.

'Green Is the Colour'

David Gilmour: guitar, vocals
Richard Wright: piano, Farfisa organ
Nick Mason: percussion
Roger Waters: lyrics, music, bass
Lindy Mason: tin whistle

Another gentle, engaging acoustic song sung, as were all the tracks on this album, by David Gilmour. Live arrangements of the song were performed as a full electric band piece and at a slower tempo. Waters' lyric uses the metaphors of sun and moon as good and evil: ideas that would be used to better effect a few years later.

Initially performed as part of *The Man and the Journey* (as 'The Beginning') between March and September 1969, 'Green Is the Colour' was performed live in its own right from September 1969 to August 1971, usually as a medley with 'Careful with That Axe, Eugene'. Three live versions were released on *The Early Years 1965–1972* box set on 2016: for BBC radio (12 May 1969), for Dutch radio (17 September 1969), and again for the BBC (16 July 1970).

'Cymbaline'

David Gilmour: guitar, vocals
Richard Wright: piano, Farfisa organ
Nick Mason: drums, bongos
Roger Waters: lyrics, music, bass

Probably the best song on *More* and something of a lost classic. Of all the songs on *More,* it survived the longest in the band's live set, until it was dropped in 1972 in favour of *The Dark Side of the Moon*. The studio cut features a sparse arrangement of nylon-string guitar, bass, piano, drums, bongos, and organ. One notable feature of the lyrics is the question posed at the end of the first verse: 'Will the final couplet rhyme?' Not coincidentally, the final couplet in the song is the only one that does not rhyme.

The version of 'Cymbaline' used in the film is a different take to this album version: some of the words are different and the organ solo is much longer.

'Cymbaline' was performed as part of *The Man and the Journey* (as 'Sleeping' or 'Nightmare') between March and September 1969, then as a track in its own right from November 1969 to November 1971. A live-in-the-studio version for BBC radio was recorded on 12 May 1969 and released on *The Early Years 1965–1972* box set in 2016, which also featured a version recorded for Dutch radio on 17 September 1969. Live versions could extend to ten minutes; a demonstration of the band's Azimuth Co-ordinator would send sounds—in this case, footsteps and door slams—to different parts of the concert hall.

'Party Sequence'

David Gilmour: music
Richard Wright: music
Roger Waters: music
Nick Mason: music, bongos
Lindy Mason: tin whistle

A penny whistle and bongos duet that is over a minute too long. The penny whistle plays the melody to 'Seabirds', a song that Pink Floyd recorded for the *More* film, but was left off the soundtrack album.

No known live performances.

'Main Theme'

Roger Waters: music, bass, gong
Richard Wright: music, Farfisa organ
David Gilmour: music, slide guitar
Nick Mason: music, drums, percussion

Released as the B-side to 'The Nile Song' in Japan.

An improvised instrumental track which sounds like it was knocked up in ten minutes, but at least it has a tune. An alternative arrangement (a faster 'beat version' with wibbly organ) was released on *The Early Years 1965–1972* box set in 2016. This piece was added to Pink Floyd's live set for six months between October 1969 and April 1970.

'Ibiza Bar'

David Gilmour: music, guitars, vocals
Richard Wright: music, piano, Farfisa organ, vocals

Roger Waters: lyrics (probable), music, bass
Nick Mason: music, drums

Released as the B-side to 'The Nile Song' in France and New Zealand.

A simple rewrite of 'The Nile Song' with heavily-echoed lead guitar and obliquely fascinating lyrics.

No known live performances.

'More Blues'

David Gilmour: music, guitar
Roger Waters: music, bass
Nick Mason: music, drums
Richard Wright: music, organ

A slow, generic blues instrumental that is not so different from those performed by bands such as Fleetwood Mac, Chicken Shack, and Savoy Brown during this period. An alternative arrangement (which is almost identical) and a BBC recording were both released in appalling sound quality on *The Early Years 1965–1972* box set in 2016.

It was performed on occasion between 1970 and 1972, most often as a 'time to go home' encore. Revived, just once, on the last date of the In the Flesh Tour: 6 July 1977 in Montreal.

'Quicksilver'

Richard Wright: music, organ, vibraphone
David Gilmour: music, guitar
Roger Waters: music, gong
Nick Mason: music, cymbals, percussion

A lengthy avant-garde instrumental, very much of its time, and no doubt evoking the sensations of a drug-induced haze. Just about unlistenable, frankly. An alternative version is available on *The Early Years 1965–1972*, listed incorrectly as 'Seabirds'.

Performed under the title 'Sleeping' as part of *The Man and the Journey*. Recorded for Dutch radio on 17 September 1969 and released on *The Early Years 1965–1972* in 2016.

'A Spanish Piece'

David Gilmour: lyrics, music, guitars, bass drum, vocals
Roger Waters: vocals

Nylon-strung guitar plonking and cod-Spanish mumbling. Pass the tequila, Manuel.

No known live performances.

'Dramatic Theme'

David Gilmour: music, guitar
Roger Waters: music, bass
Nick Mason: music, drums
Richard Wright: music, Farfisa organ

A slowed-down version of the opening section of 'Let There Be More Light'. There is some interesting guitar work from David Gilmour, but very little to engage the listener.

No known live performances.

Unused Tracks

'Hollywood'

Written by David Gilmour.

Very much in the same vein as the rest of the *More* album, with acoustic guitar, and using some of the same chords changes as 'Cymbaline': a twisty lead guitar part and simple organ.

'Seabirds'

Written by Roger Waters.

Listed as appearing on *The Early Years 1965–1972* box set, but the track used seems to be an alternative take of 'Quicksilver'.

Review

> The group's atmospheric music was a natural for movies, but when assembled for record, these pieces were unavoidably a bit patchwork, ranging from folky ballads to fierce electronic instrumentals to incidental mood music.
>
> AllMusic

Ummagumma (1969)

Live tracks recorded 27 April 1969 at the Mothers Club, Birmingham and 2 May 1969 at Manchester College of Commerce. Studio tracks recorded summer 1969, probably at EMI Studios, Abbey Road, London. Produced by Pink Floyd and Norman Smith. First released 25 October 1969 (UK: Harvest SHDW1/2) and 10 November 1969 (US: Capitol SKBB-388).

Ummagumma was an unusual, not wholly successful, experiment—half live recordings and half solo studio recordings. The album was quite possibly something of a risk, coming so soon after the half-hearted *More* album, which had been released only four months previously.

> We were at a loose end with *Ummagumma*. We didn't know what the fuck else to do.
>
> David Gilmour, interview with Mark Blake (2008)

Throughout 1969, Pink Floyd had been performing a two-part suite called *The Man and the Journey*. The suite consisted of several of their early songs, some unreleased songs, and material later included on *More* and *Ummagumma,* including 'Grantchester Meadows' and parts of both 'The Narrow Way' and 'The Grand Vizier's Garden Party'. These three were recorded for *Ummagumma*, with other new songs, once the main part of the tour had concluded at the end of June 1969.

Whereas the studio recordings will receive infrequent listens from even the most devout Floyd fan, the robust live recordings stood the test of time as the only officially released live recordings of Pink Floyd before 1988.[1]

Ummagumma was the first Floyd album to break the Top 100 album chart in the United States, peaking at number seventy-four and was a Top 5 album in the UK.

The cassette edition of the album completely re-orders the tracks, removing the live/ studio split.

Side 1: 'Sysyphus' / 'Astronomy Domine' / 'Grantchester Meadows' / 'Several Species of Small Furry Animals Gathered Together in a Cave and Grooving with a Pict' / 'Careful with That Axe, Eugene'.
Side 2: 'The Narrow Way' / 'Set the Controls for the Heart of the Sun' / The Grand Vizier's Garden Party / 'A Saucerful of Secrets'.

'Astronomy Domine'
Recorded 27 April 1969 at the Mothers Club, Birmingham
'Careful with That Axe, Eugene'
Recorded 2 May 1969 at Manchester College of Commerce
'Set the Controls for the Heart of the Sun'
Recorded 2 May 1969 at Manchester College of Commerce

'A Saucerful of Secrets'
Recorded 27 April 1969 at the Mothers Club, Birmingham

Fabulous, wonderfully recorded live versions of four tracks from the band's current set-list, in every case a vast sonic and dynamic improvement on their studio versions.

The original intention was to release these songs so that the band no longer needed to play them in concert. However, with the popularity of the *Ummagumma*, the public kept wanting to hear songs from the live album, and so they stayed in their set lists for some time: 'Astronomy Domine' would remain part of the set until the end of 1971, while the other three would be staples right through until the end of 1973.

'Interstellar Overdrive' was also recorded for the album but remains unreleased. It is a shame that room was not found for this outtake on the otherwise exhaustive *The Early Years 1965–1972* box set.

'Sysyphus (Parts 1–4)'

Richard Wright: music, all instruments

An avant-garde and occasionally illuminating, if overlong, instrumental four-part suite written and performed by Richard Wright

There were four known performances of 'Sysyphus', all between November 1969 and February 1970.

'Grantchester Meadows'

Roger Waters: lyrics, music, guitars, vocals

'Grantchester Meadows', named after an area in Waters' home town of Cambridge, is perhaps the most successful song on the *Ummagumma* studio album. However, the lengthy birdsong, insect, and footsteps effects do not merit repeated listenings. Live performances included Gilmour on a second acoustic guitar and harmony vocals during the chorus, as well as Richard Wright playing two piano solos.

'Grantchester Meadows' was first performed as part of *The Man and the Journey* concert suite throughout 1969. A live-in-the-studio version with a disjointed piano solo was recorded for BBC Radio on 12 May 1969, and released on *The Early Years 1965–1972* box set in 2016. The song was also recorded for Dutch radio on 17 September 1969, and likewise released on *The Early Years 1965-1972*.

'Several Species of Small Furry Animals Gathered Together in a Cave and Grooving with a Pict'

Roger Waters: composition, vocals

Waters creates the sounds of woodland creatures and rants in a Scottish accent for much longer than is necessary. The only thing worth mentioning is the reversed message toward the end which says, 'That was pretty avant-garde, wasn't it?'

Some sources suggest that Waters' pal Ron Geesin provides the titular pict, but Geesin has apparently refuted this.

There are a handful of live performances of this piece, included as part of renditions of 'Sysyphus', between November 1969 and February 1970. The album cut is infinitely more listenable.

'The Narrow Way (Parts 1–3)'

David Gilmour: lyrics, music, guitars, vocals, bass, piano, organ, drums

> I just went into a studio and started waffling about, tacking bits and pieces together. I haven't heard it in years. I've no idea what it's like.
>
> David Gilmour, *Sounds Guitar Heroes* (1983)

Part 1 of this song, an aimless acoustic guitar jam, was performed for the BBC on 2 December 1968. At that time it was called 'Baby Blue Shuffle in D minor', and this version can be heard on *The Early Years 1965–1972* box set. Part 2 features an electric guitar playing a simple riff over percussion sounds, eventually modulating into a drone. Part 3 is an actual song, and a reasonably good one at that, with a strong vocal melody from Gilmour and an uplifting conclusion.

Part 3 of 'The Narrow Way' was performed throughout 1969 as part of *The Man and the Journey* suite. A live-in-the-studio version for BBC Radio was recorded on 12 May 1969 and released on *The Early Years 1965–1972* box set in 2016; the box set also contains a recording for Dutch radio from 17 September 1969.

'The Grand Vizier's Garden Party (Part 1: Entrance; Part 2: Entertainment; Part 3: Exit)'

Nick Mason: composition, drums, timpani, percussion, Mellotron, xylophone
Lindy Mason: flute

This is a seven-minute drum solo with some flutes.

The 'Entertainment' section of 'The Grand Vizier's Garden Party' was one of a number tracks which were played at some point in the *The Man and the Journey* suite under the name 'Doing It'. Others included 'Up the Khyber' and 'Party Sequence' (from *More*) and 'Syncopated Pandemonium' (from *A Saucerful of Secrets*).

> Casual fans who love 'Wish You Were Here' and 'Money' may not find much to love here, but to the truly devoted *Ummagumma* is Pink Floyd at the peak of their ambitious weirdness.
>
> Rolling Stone, Top 10 Pink Floyd albums (September 2013)

> The studio material on the second disc corrals some convoluted suites by Nick Mason and Richard Wright, who aren't frontmen for a very good reason. Their multi-section compositions meander noisily and pointlessly, with none of the kinetic din of their previous material. Looking for transcendence in synthobirds and what sounds like monkeys cavorting in a Steinway showroom, they mistake aimlessness for import, in the process creating a towering monument to rock self-indulgence.
>
> Stephen Deusner, *Paste Monthly* (September 2011)

Other Related Material

'Biding My Time'

Roger Waters: lyrics, music, bass, vocals
David Gilmour: guitars
Richard Wright: piano, organ, trombone
Nick Mason: drums, percussion

Recorded in July 1969, 'Biding My Time' would not be released for another two years, when it would be the only new track on the compilation album *Relics*. It is a straightforward slow blues, moving into an up-tempo second section with a trombone solo (played by Richard Wright) and furious guitar (Gilmour).

'Biding My Time' was performed throughout 1969 under the title 'Afternoon', as part of *The Man and the Journey* suite. It was recorded for Dutch radio on 17 September 1969 and released on *The Early Years 1965–1972* in 2016.

'Work'

Percussion and vibraphone, part of *The Man and the Journey*. Recorded for Dutch radio on 17 September 1969 and released on *The Early Years 1965–1972* in 2016.

'Labyrinth'

A ticking clock sound effect used at the end of 'Nightmare' (aka 'Cymbeline') within *The Man and the Journey*, the conclusion to *The Man* part of this concept. The entire suite was recorded for Dutch radio on 17 September 1969 and released on *The Early Years 1965–1972* in 2016.

'Embryo'

David Gilmour: guitars, vocals
Richard Wright: Mellotron, Farfisa organa, piano
Roger Waters: lyrics, music, bass
Nick Mason: drums, percussion

Written in late 1968 and performed for the BBC that December, 'Embryo' was a reflective, starkly poetic song which would have fitted neatly onto side two of *Atom Heart Mother*.

It was recorded at Abbey Road on 3 June 1969. The song was never completed in the studio, but was released in June 1970, without the band's agreement, on a sampler album called *Picnic—A Breath of Fresh Air*. This same version was included on *Works*, a 1983 Canadian compilation, this time with the band's agreement. The 1969 recording was made more widely available on *The Early Years 1965–1972* twenty-eight-disc box set in 2016.

'Embryo' was recorded for the BBC on 20 December 1968. It was then performed in a more 'rock' arrangement, often lasting for 12 minutes—sometimes much longer—throughout 1970 and 1971. The BBC recording was also released on *The Early Years 1965–1972* box set. A second longer and louder in-concert recording for the BBC (30 September 1971) was included in the same release.

'Moonhead'

Recorded on 10 July 1969 for the BBC to play in-between broadcast coverage of the first Apollo moon landing on the 20th. It was released, seemingly taken directly from the broadcast itself, on *The Early Years 1965–1972* box set in 2016, and is very reminiscent in places of the songs 'Cirrus Minor' and 'Main Theme' from *More*.

The only known public performance was as part of a twenty-four-minute experimental piece which also included 'Heart Beat Pig Meat', 'Quicksilver', and 'The Violent Sequence' (an early version of 'Us and Them'). This piece has been released on the bootleg *Project Birmingham*.

'Corrosion in the Pink Room'

Written by Waters, Gilmour, Wright, and Mason.

An instrumental piece that was played at live shows during the early 1970s. It is a very avant-garde piece, with eerie piano playing by Wright and scatting by Waters, reminiscent of the sounds on 'Several Species of Small Furry Animals Gathered Together in a Cave and Grooving with a Pict'. Halfway through, the song transitions to a jazzy blues jam, similar to 'Funky Dung' from 'Atom Heart Mother'.

Zabriskie Point (1970)

Recorded in Rome, 16 November 1969, 6 December 1969, and 12 December 1969.

First released 30 May 1970 (UK: MGM-CS-8120) and 12 April 1970 (US: MGM SE-4668ST), it was rereleased with extra tracks in 1997 (2 x CD, Rhino R2 72 462), and another sixteen outtakes were made available in 2016.

Pink Floyd travelled to Rome at the end of 1969 to record several pieces of music for the soundtrack of the Michelangelo Antonioni film *Zabriskie Point*.

'Heart Beat, Pig Meat'

Written by Roger Waters, David Gilmour, Richard Wright, and Nick Mason.

This is typical of the repetitive instrumentals that filled most of *More* and *Ummagumma*. The voices and sound effects, however, look forward to *The Dark Side of the Moon* and *The Wall*.

The only known live performance of 'Heart Beat, Pig Meat' is in the opening section to a twenty-four-minute experimental piece which also included 'Quicksilver', 'Moonhead' and 'The Violent Sequence' (an early version of 'Us and Them'). This piece has been released on the *Project Birmingham* bootleg.

'Crumbling Land'

Written by Roger Waters, David Gilmour, Richard Wright, and Nick Mason.

This song is not so far from the music of the Grateful Dead and Kaleidoscope, who also provided songs for the film. Apart from Richard Wright's wide-apart piano chords, it does not sound much like Pink Floyd.

No known live performances.

'Come in Number 51, Your Time Is Up'

Written by Roger Waters, David Gilmour, Richard Wright, and Nick Mason.\

A cryptically-titled remake of the Floyd's volcanic 1968 B-side 'Careful with That Axe, Eugene'. Its roaring guitars, crashing drums, and death throe screaming are the perfect complement to the film's cataclysmic finish.

Bonus Tracks Released in 1997 and 2016

Another twenty tracks from these sessions were released in 1997 and 2016 as part of the CD rerelease of the soundtrack album and *The Early Years 1965–1972* box set. Surprisingly, these outtakes are generally excellent. There are no known live performances of any of these songs.

'Auto Scene Version 2' / 'Auto Scene Version 3'

'Auto Scene Version 2' is a faster, instrumental version of 'Rain in the Country'.

'Auto Scene Version 3' is a basic three-chord vamp driven by Wright's organ.

'Love Scene (Take 1)' / 'Love Scene (Take 2)' / 'Love Scene Version 1' / 'Love Scene Version 2' / 'Love Scene (Version 4)' / 'Love Scene Version 6' / 'Love Scene Version 7' / 'Unknown Song (Take 1)' / 'Unknown Song (Rain in the Country)'

'Love Scene (Take 1)' is a tasteful jazzy piano-led meandering with vibraphone

'Love Scene (Take 2)' is a vibraphone work-out.

'Love Scene Version 1', often listed on Pink Floyd bootlegs under the title 'Oenone' or 'Oneone', is a very stark, almost ambient organ piece.

'Love Scene Version 2' is a lovely, slow, and atmospheric instrumental with organ and spacey guitar.

'Love Scene (Version 4)' is lounge jazz.

'Love Scene Version 6' is a bluesy instrumental listed as 'Alan's Blues' on some bootlegs.

'Love Scene Version 7' is an exquisite acoustic instrumental, not so far from the first part of 'The Narrow Way' and the later 'A Pillow of Winds'—'Unknown Song (Take 1)' and 'Unknown Song (Rain in the Country)' are reworkings of this.

'Country Song'

'Country Song' is a straightforward country rewrite of 'Green is the Colour', featuring honky-tonk piano by Richard Wright;

'Take Off' / 'Take Off Version 2'

'Take Off' is a surprisingly aggressive guitar and drums instrumental which could be an *Animals* outtake.

'Take Off Version 2' is a muscular rock instrumental that would have made a great song.

'Aeroplane' / 'Crumbling Land (Take 1)' / 'On the Highway'

'Aeroplane' is a raucously riffed blues instrumental, with Gilmour employing his best Hendrix impression.

Meanwhile 'On the Highway' is a shortened, more acoustic version of 'Crumbling Land', which contrasts with 'Crumbling Land (Take 1)': a more urgent take, faster and busier.

'Explosion' / 'Looking at the Map' / 'The Riot Scene'

'Explosion' is a bluesy variation on 'Careful With That Axe, Eugene', using Waters' then favourite bass line, borrowed from concurrent live versions of that piece.

'Looking at the Map' is another, rather lovely version of 'Rain in the Country', this one with some tasteful guitar picking and Gilmour vocalisations.

Finally, 'The Riot Scene' is the piano-only demo of 'Us and Them', previously released on the Immersion box set of *The Dark Side of the Moon*.

Review

> Having commissioned Pink Floyd to provide the soundtrack in late 1969, an unimpressed Antonioni included only three of their songs in the film. Yet from such inauspicious beginnings, the soundtrack to Zabriskie Point captures the dystopic mood of late 60s California in the same way as Performance reflects the murk of London. Anyone who's seen the use of 'Come in Number 51, Your Time Is Up' in the final climactic scene in Death Valley will know that as rock soundtracks go, *Zabriskie Point* is unforgettable.
>
> Paul Moody, The Guardian (July 2007)

Atom Heart Mother (1970)

Recorded February–August 1970 at EMI Studios, Abbey Road, London. Produced by Pink Floyd. Executive producer: Norman Smith. First released on 2 October 1970 (UK: Harvest SHVL 781; US: Harvest SKAO-382).

Pink Floyd start to emerge from Syd Barrett's shadow.

Back in London after their experience in Rome recording the soundtrack to *Zabriskie Point* in November and December 1969, Pink Floyd started working on material for their fifth album. A twenty-three-minute piece was built up from various semi-improvised segments, with the main theme being based around a David Gilmour chord progression derived from Elmer Bernstein's theme music to *The Magnificent Seven* (1960). This as-yet-untitled instrumental was first performed at Hull University on 17 January 1970. Recording of the piece took several weeks in early March and, after a European tour, the backing track was completed in late March and early April. The band toured the US in May, leaving composer Ron Geesin to create a score for brass and choir, before returning to the studio for further sessions in June and July, recording the songs that made up side two of their new album. With its iconic sleeve, featuring the rear end of Lulubelle III, *Atom Heart Mother* was one of the first albums by a major label band to not include the artist's name on the front cover.

> Rather than being a prog-rock indulgence, *Atom Heart Mother* is a rather humble, almost down-to-earth affair [that] oozes a summery, pastoral, lazy, faintly melancholy joyfulness.
>
> Mark Blake, *Pigs Might Fly: The inside Story of Pink Floyd* (2007)

For Floyd train spotters, it would be during the second set of sessions for *Atom Heart Mother* that David Gilmour first used his famous black Stratocaster guitar. It would be his principal in-studio and on-stage guitar until 1985, and again from 2005 onwards.[2]

Atom Heart Mother was Pink Floyd's first UK No. 1 album.

'Atom Heart Mother'

David Gilmour: music, guitars, slide guitar
Roger Waters: music, bass
Richard Wright: music, Hammond organ, Farfisa organ, Mellotron, piano
Nick Mason: music, drums, percussion
Ron Geesin: music, conductor
Haflidi Hallgrimsson: cello
The John Alldis Choir:
  Eleanor Capp, Jessica Cash, Rosemary Hardy, Hazel Holt: soprano vocals
  Margaret Cable, Peggy Castle, Meriel Dickinson, Lynne Hurst, Geoffrey Mitchell, Celia Piercy, Patricia Sabin: alto vocals
  Rogers Covey-Crump, Peter Hall, John Whitworth, Kenneth Woolham: tenor vocals
  John Huw Davies, Brian Etheridge, Bryn Evans, Brian Kay: baritone vocals
  David Thomas: bass vocals
  John Alldis: conductor, arranger
EMI Pops Orchestra: three trumpets, three horns, three trombones, a tuba, two violins, two woodwind

Pink Floyd's first side-length composition is flawed and repetitive, but ultimately a triumph. Early live performances show that the piece was unfocused and was missing something. It had been written during the early part of January 1970. The backing track (titled 'Epic' at that time) was recorded back at EMI Studios, Abbey Road in March and April 1970. A recording of the song at this stage in its development was released on *The Early Years 1965–1970* box set in 2016.

This recording was subsequently handed to musician and composer Ron Geesin. Geesin had been friendly with Nick Mason for eighteen months or so, and it was at one of Mason's dinner parties in 1969 that Geesin met Roger Waters.[3] Early in 1970, Geesin and Waters agreed to write and perform the music for the film *The Body*; recording would progress intermittently through 1970, either side of sessions for *Atom Heart Mother.*[4]

> One side is a complete 25-minute piece on which we are using other musicians for the first time. We decided it would be nice to use a choir and a brass section. None of us writes music so we approached Ron Geesin, who is a friend of ours, and asked him if he'd like to be involved.
>
> Roger Waters, quoted in *New Musical Express* (4 July 1970)

> It would have been around March that Nick and Roger first asked me if I would do anything with a tape they had compiled at Abbey Road. They wanted 'something big'. It is most likely that I was given a rough mix sometime between 22 March and 8 April 1970. Pink Floyd did not provide any drawn up map of the construction, not even the chords in their sequences. We sorted out what would be needed to achieve 'something big' and my vision of contrasting moods and melodies. The choice [was] ten brass, twenty choir and solo cello.
>
> Ron Geesin in *The Flaming Cow: The Making of Pink Floyd's Atom Heart Mother* (2013)

Geesin spent most of May transcribing Pink Floyd's backing track while the band toured the US. Wright and Gilmour swapped ideas with Geesin in the last week of May and overdub sessions were booked for the following month, allowing Geesin just three weeks to write his score.

Recording commenced at Abbey Road on 19 June 1970. The sessions were not without their problems, as Geesin struggled to reconcile the orchestral score with the wavering tempo of Pink Floyd's backing track. Geesin eventually threw in the towel and choir-master John Aldiss would subsequently supervise the remaining overdub sessions. The resultant twenty-three-minute piece balances Pink Floyd's four-piece line-up against strident horns, a wordless twenty-piece choir, an avant-garde interlude, and a beautiful cello melody.

The six sections listed on the album sleeve are 'Father's Shout', 'Breast Milky', 'Mother

Fore', 'Funky Dung', 'Mind Your Throats Please', and 'Remergence', determined from a combination of suggestions by Geesin and Pink Floyd.

These break down as follows:

00:00–2:52: 'Father's Shout'—a stuttering horn introduction, the emergence of the main theme and a development of that main theme with Western sound effects and a roaring motorcycle

2:52–5:22: 'Breast Milky'—a beautiful duet for organ and cello leads into a rousing section, with Gilmour's slide guitar cutting through the strident drums and horns

5:22—10:11: 'Mother Fore'—a lengthy choral section, with wordless voices offering counterpoint to Mason's busy drum fills

10:11—14:56: 'Funky Dung'—a wide-open bluesy guitar solo against a leaping bass and fat organ chords[5]

14:56—19:11: 'Mind Your Throats, Please'—a reprise of the main theme, then a collage of tape effects, sometimes reminiscent of The Beatles' 'Revolution #9'

19:11—23:44: 'Remergence'—a further development of the main theme with brass, a reprise of the cello/organ duet, and some spacey slide guitar takes us to another reprise of the main theme, with brass and choir and a tremendous final chord which is the aural equivalent of the sun busting through the clouds on a stormy day.[6]

For the first time, we hear David Gilmour's guitar phrasing moving beyond his blues roots. Gilmour's expressive note-bends and sustained tone would be a key element of his performance style in the forthcoming 'Echoes', 'Money', 'Shine on You Crazy Diamond', 'Dogs', 'Comfortably Numb', and 'Marooned'. The double-tracked harmonic guitars in 'Remergence' are particularly effective, as Gilmour is finally allowed to let loose.

> It wasn't how I envisioned it, but it was a good compromise. I wanted more punch, but then again the Floyd always seemed to need that pastel wash on their music.
>
> Ron Geesin, quoted in *Pigs Might Fly: The Inside Story of Pink Floyd* (2007)

> I think ['Atom Heart Mother' is] a pretty flawed, weak track and I don't diverge from that view.
>
> David Gilmour, interview with Mark Blake (2008)

As recorded, the piece was without a formal title, but was sometimes called 'The Amazing Pudding' until Pink Floyd performed for the BBC on 16 July 1970, and Roger Waters picked a headline from *The Evening Standard*.

The piece was first performed in Hull on 17 January 1970, with the first performance with brass and choir at the Bath Festival on 27 June 1970.[7] Live versions for the BBC on 16 July 1970 (with brass and choir) and at Montreux on 21 November 1970 (without brass and choir) were released on *The Early Years 1965–1970*. A later arrangement was pared down from twenty-five minutes to fifteen, and remained in the band's live repertoire into 1972, with the last known performance in Amsterdam on 22 May 1972.

'If'

Roger Waters: lyrics, music, vocals, guitar, bass guitar
David Gilmour: slide guitar
Richard Wright: piano, Hammond organ
Nick Mason: drums

The four quiet, contemplative, mostly acoustic songs on side two of *Atom Heart Mother* balance the epic scale of the long, complex title track on side one.

Waters' introspective and reflective acoustic ballad 'If' provides some of his best lyrical expression to date: it is in the same vein as (but a marked improvement on) 'Grantchester Meadows', and a definite precursor to the themes explored on *The Dark Side of the Moon*.

'If' was performed only once, for the BBC (prior to being recorded at EMI) on 16 July 1970; this was released on *The Early Years 1965–1970*.

'Summer '68'

Richard Wright: lyrics, music, vocals, piano, Hammond organ
David Gilmour: guitars, vocals
Roger Waters: bass
Nick Mason: drums, percussion
The Abbey Road Session Pops Orchestra

Surely Richard Wright's best solo composition, the wistful, heartfelt 'Summer '68' relates Wright's memories of the band's first US tour in a style that is far, far from 'Sysyphus' and 'Atom Heart Mother'.

Very rare for Pink Floyd, the subject matter is sex, reflecting Wright's emptiness following a liaison with a groupie. Exploration of human emotions would play a much larger role in Pink Floyd's music from now on.

Wright's 'How do you feel?' refrain shares the melody and most of the words to the opening line of Roy Harper's 'How Does It Feel?' from his album *Flat Baroque and Berserk*, released at the beginning of 1970. Harper and Pink Floyd both performed on the same bill at Hyde Park on 18 July 1970.

This song also has a well-known misheard lyric toward the end. According to the CD reissue of *Atom Heart Mother*, the lyrics are 'Goodbye to you, Charlotte Pringle's due'. I am not sure who Charlotte Pringle is—a 'historic figure in the UK' if we believe one online source. The correct lyrics, as seen in the *Atom Heart Mother* sheet music published in 1980, are 'Goodbye to you, childlike bangles, too'. Which, of course, fits perfectly into the meaning of the song.

No known live performances.

'Fat Old Sun'

David Gilmour: lyrics, music, vocals, guitars, pedal steel guitar, bass, drums, percussion
Richard Wright: Farfisa organ, Hammond organ

Distant church bells and a languid acoustic guitar usher in a lazy, bucolic, summer-evening feeling. Essentially a very English retread of West Coast acts such as Crosby, Stills, and Nash, 'Fat Old Sun' is one of those almost-classic tracks that displays the depth and breadth of the Pink Floyd back catalogue.

In live performances, 'Fat Old Sun' would be played by the whole band in a much louder, longer electric arrangement—the antithesis of the gentle acoustic feel of the studio version.

First performed for the BBC, prior to being recorded at EMI, on 16 July 1970, this acoustic version was released on *The Early Years 1965–1970* in 2016. A second, longer, electric version was recorded for the BBC on 30 September 1971, and included in the same box set. 'Fat Old Sun' was subsequently performed in concert until the end of 1971, when it was dropped to make way for *The Dark Side of the Moon*. It was also performed by Pink Floyd at manager Steve O'Rourke's funeral in Chichester Cathedral in 2003, and by David Gilmour on his 2006 and 2015–2016 solo tours.[8]

'Alan's Psychedelic Breakfast'

David Gilmour: music, guitars
Roger Waters: music, bass
Richard Wright: music, piano, Hammond organ
Nick Mason: music, drums, percussion
Alan Styles: voice[9]

'Alan's Psychedelic Breakfast' is divided into three musical segments: 'Rise and Shine', 'Sunny Side Up', and 'Morning Glory', linked by dialogue and sound effects of then-roadie Alan Styles preparing, discussing, and eating breakfast.

What sounds like an unbearable conceit is both charming and entertaining—careful editing of the non-musical elements into the sometimes-lightweight instrumental tunes brings the best out of both, resulting in an unexpected and surprisingly satisfying listening experience. The sound effects and spoken interludes of 'Alan's Psychedelic Breakfast' look forward to *The Dark Side of the Moon*, two years hence.

It was performed only four times: in Birmingham, Bristol, Manchester, and Sheffield between 18–22 December 1970.

Reviews

As a whole it's awful schmaltzy and a little vapid. Side two is generally worse. It is English folk at its deadly worst. It's soft and silly. If Pink Floyd is looking for some new dimensions, they haven't found them here.

Alec Dubro, *Rolling Stone* (December 1970)

Roger Waters and David Gilmour have spent 40 years playing this 1970 album down, labelling it pompous, overblown, embarrassing. They're not exactly wrong, but they're not exactly right either. But *Atom Heart Mother* shows the band developing and entertaining new ideas, consciously moving away from the space rock label they'd been saddled with.

Stephen Deusner, *Paste Monthly* (October 2011)

3

Floyd Phase 3: 1971–1975 Four Star Day Dream

Meddle (1971)

Recorded January 1971 at EMI Studios, Abbey Road, London; March–July 1971 at Morgan Sound Studios, London; July–August 1971 at AIR Studios, London. First released 5 November 1971 (UK: SHVL 795); 30 October 1971 (US: SMAS-832)

At last, the real Pink Floyd stand up.

At a time when major artists might release a new album every four or five years, it seems astonishing that Pink Floyd, as was common in the music industry at the time, would not only record and promote new albums annually, but also maintain a high level of artistic integrity with each release.

Touring constantly to promote *Atom Heart Mother* between September–December 1970, Pink Floyd convened at David Gilmour's London home a few days before Christmas, and agreed to work together to write and rehearse a new piece over the coming weeks. Off the road for most of January 1971, this new twenty-three-minute piece, as then untitled but later called 'Echoes', was premiered in Norwich on 22 April 1971. 'Echoes' was recorded in gaps in the band's 1971 touring schedule and, as with 'Atom Heart Mother', would fill an entire side of an album.

> We were looking for something. During that whole period through *Ummagumma* and *Atom Heart Mother* we were finding ourselves. 'Echoes' was the point at which we found our focus.
>
> David Gilmour, quoted in *Pigs Might Fly: The Inside Story of Pink Floyd* (2007)

Released exactly one year after *Atom Heart Mother*, *Meddle* would solidify Pink Floyd's reputation as major recording artists, and herald the start of their much-admired and hugely successful 'mid-period', comprising this and their next four albums.

A remixed 5.1 version of the entire album was released as a hidden Easter egg on *The Early Years 1965–1972* in 2016.

'One of These Days'

David Gilmour: music, guitars, pedal steel guitar, bass (left channel)
Roger Waters: music, bass (right channel)
Nick Mason: music, drums, backwards cymbals, vocals
Richard Wright: music, Hammond organ, piano, EMS VCS 3 synthesiser

Recorded 19-21 July, 23-25 July 1971 at Morgan Sound Studios, London and released as a single in the US (29 November 1971), and in Italy and Japan (1971).

Pink Floyd's sixth album opens with a double-tracked pair of thundering bass guitars. Roger Waters put his instrument through an echo unit, then played along with the repeated notes, inspiring David Gilmour to pick up a second bass and join in. Mason provides one of his best drumming performances to drive the piece along.[1] Wright adds some surging organ chords as musical exclamation marks. The finishing touch is the overdubbing of Gilmour's huge, furious, distorted lap steel guitar which cuts through and hovers above the enormous rhythm section.

In many ways, 'One of These Days' is a souped-up 'Careful with That Axe, Eugene': an exercise in dynamics mostly on a single chord, but executed with skill and, for once, economy.

'One of These Days' was an in-concert regular between 1971 and 1973. The song's live debut was at the Paris Theatre, London, on 30 September 1971 for BBC *In Concert*, available for years on the famous bootleg *Meddled* and ultimately included in *The Early Years 1965–1972* box set. A superb live-without-an-audience version was recorded in Pompeii for *Live in Pompeii* between 4–7 October 1971, and this was also released on *The Early Years 1965–1972* in 2016. The song was revived in 1987 and played at every full-length concert in Pink Floyd's 1987–1989 and 1994 tours. A live version recorded at Nassau Coliseum between 19–23 August 1988 is available on *Delicate Sound of Thunder* (22 November 1988). A live version recorded at Niedersachsenstadion, Hannover, on 17 August 1994 is available on the *High Hopes* CD single (17 October 1994); a second live version from this tour, recorded 21 October 1994 at Earl's Court, is available on the vinyl and cassette versions of *P•U•L•S•E* (29 May 1995).

'A Pillow of Winds'

David Gilmour: music, vocals, guitars, slide guitars, pedal steel guitar
Richard Wright: Hammond organ, piano
Nick Mason: hi-hat
Roger Waters: lyrics, bass

Recorded July 1971 at Morgan Sound Studios, London.

The latest in a series of acoustic ballads that provide much-needed contrast from Pink Floyd's heavier pieces, 'A Pillow of Winds' is a mellow song, mostly performed and sung by a sleepy-sounding Gilmour on a single chord. Part of the central guitar melody and the fretless bass pattern were later re-used in the song 'Hey You' from *The Wall*.

The song's title originates from a hand in the game of mah-jong, with which the band killed time while touring.

No known live performances.

'Fearless'

David Gilmour: lyrics, music, guitars, vocals
Roger Waters: lyrics, music, bass
Richard Wright: piano
Nick Mason: drums, percussion

Recorded July 1971 at Morgan Sound Studios, London and released as the B-side of 'One of These Days' in the US (29 November 1971) and Italy (1971).

Lyrically a precursor to 'Brain Damage' ('Fearlessly the idiot faced the crowd / The lunatic is on the grass'), 'Fearless' employs a droning open G acoustic guitar chording, a wistful vocal from Gilmour, a typically knotty Waters lyric and a lightly tapped drum pattern from Nick Mason. The overdubbed chanting of 'You'll Never Walk Alone' recorded at Liverpool FC is a droll in-joke achieved by production trickery.[2]

There are no confirmed live performances by Pink Floyd, but the song was unexpectedly revived by Roger Waters on his 2016 live dates.

'San Tropez'

Roger Waters: lyrics, music, guitar, bass, vocals
David Gilmour: slide guitar
Richard Wright: piano
Nick Mason: drums, percussion

Recorded August 1971 at Morgan Sound Studios, London.

More late-night lounge jazz from Roger Waters as he gives us an idealised vision of what a day in the south of France might be like. It includes a very basic slide guitar solo from David Gilmour and one-finger piano break from Richard Wright. Waters' lyric hints at the seeds of a clash between his rock 'n' roll lifestyle and his socialist upbringing that would see full flower later in the decade: 'I'm drinking champagne like a good tycoon'.

> Roger came in and the song was absolutely complete. There was almost no arranging to do on it. It was just a matter of learning the chords.
>
> Nick Mason, quoted in *New Musical Express* (19 February 1972)

No known live performances.

'Seamus'

David Gilmour: lyrics, music, guitar, harmonica, vocals
Roger Waters: music, bass
Richard Wright: music, piano
Nick Mason: music
Seamus: 'vocals'

Recorded July–August 1971 at Morgan Sound Studios, London and released as the B-side of 'One of These Days' in Japan in 1971.

Most certainly a joke and quite a good one, as Gilmour's stoned throwaway cod-blues complete with howling dog lightens the mood.[3]

There is supposedly one known public live performance, at the Park Center, Charlotte, NC, on 23 March 1973 during *The Dark Side of the Moon* tour—but this seems unlikely, and recorded proof is not forthcoming.

'Echoes'

David Gilmour: music, vocals, guitars
Richard Wright: music, vocals, Hammond organ, Farfisa organ, grand piano
Roger Waters: lyrics, music, bass
Nick Mason: music, drums, percussion

Recorded January 1971 at EMI Studios, Abbey Road, London; March–June and July 1971 at Morgan Sound Studios, London.

Regarded by many as the best Pink Floyd track of all time, 'Echoes' continues the tradition of piecing together disparate musical elements, as in 'A Saucerful of Secrets' and 'Atom Heart Mother', but does so with a confidence, dynamism, power and musicality absent from these earlier works. The fifty-eight seconds from 18:14 to 19:12 comprise one of the finest pieces of music that this band ever created.

'Echoes' starts with the sound of a single note of Richard Wright's piano through an echo unit, producing a submarine-like ping.

> The idea was always to create a continuous piece of music that went through various

> moods and this was the album that established that. Rick was the guy who got it off the ground with that one note at the beginning.
>
> Nick Mason, *Mojo* (May 1994)

> As crystalline as icy water droplets on a rock.
>
> Toby Manning, *The Rough Guide to Pink Floyd* (2006)

The structure of 'Echoes' is the first time that Pink Floyd take an essentially simple song; define it within one or two verses after an extended introduction; lengthen through semi-jammed, but technically proficient instrumental passages; then deconstruct the entire piece, only to rebuild to a moody resolution via a repeat of the verse. This same technique would be used to great effect on later compositions such as 'Shine On You Crazy Diamond'; 'Dogs'; and, in a more compact form, on 'Money'. A work in progress recording of the song, comprising the chord progression that opens the second half of the released piece, was included on *The Early Years 1965–1972* box set.

> The guitar sound in the middle section of 'Echoes' was created inadvertently by David plugging in a wah-wah pedal back to front. Sometimes great effects are the results of this kind of pure serendipity and we were always prepared to see if something might work on a track.
>
> Nick Mason in *Inside Out: A Personal History of Pink Floyd* (2004)

> ['Echoes' is] a composition of unprecedented power and imagination. [In] a passage immediately before the final reprise of the first section the Floyd achieved a quite unprecedented synthesis of dexterity and sheer musical power.
>
> John Harris, *The Dark Side of the Moon: The Making of Pink Floyd's Masterpiece* (2005)

'Echoes' is one of the key tracks in Pink Floyd's entire oeuvre—a true classic and a cornerstone of their live set for the next four years.

> 'Echoes' is both prog Pink Floyd's peak and its last post. For while there would be further epics, experiments and studio longeurs in the future, never would Pink Floyd again sound like a band operating outside the musical mainstream.
>
> Toby Manning, *The Rough Guide to Pink Floyd* (2006)

The first live performance of 'Echoes' was at the Norwich Lads Club on 22 April 1971. It was recorded in London for BBC's *In Concert* radio programme on 30 September

1971, available on *The Early Years 1965–1972* box set. The following week, 'Echoes' was performed in Pompeii for the *Live in Pompeii* film—also available on *The Early Years 1965–1972*—and it remained a constant in the band's set until 1975.[4] A third version, recorded for the BBC at Wembley in 1974, was included on *The Early Years.*[5] 'Echoes' was briefly revived during the early weeks of the *A Momentary Lapse of Reason* tour in 1987, and by David Gilmour for his *On An Island* tour in 2006.

Review

> *Meddle* not only confirms lead guitarist David Gilmour's emergence as a real shaping force with the group, it states forcefully and accurately that the group is well into the growth track again. 'Echoes', a 23-minute Pink Floyd aural extravaganza that takes up all of side two, recaptures, within a new musical framework, some of the old themes and melody lines from earlier albums. All of this plus a funky organ-bass-drums segment and a stunning Gilmour solo adds up to a fine extended electronic outing. *Meddle* is killer Floyd from start to finish.

Jean-Charles Costa, *Rolling Stone* (January 1972)

Obscured by Clouds (1972)

Recorded from 23–29 February and 23 March–6 April 1972 at Strawberry Studios, Château d'Hérouville, Hérouville, Île-de-France, France. Produced by Pink Floyd. First released 2 June 1972 (UK: Harvest SHSP 4020); 15 June 1972 (US: Harvest ST-11078ST)

This was Pink Floyd's second soundtrack for Barbet Schroeder, this time for the French film *La Vallée*.

Under extreme time pressure to write and record ten new songs—Pink Floyd had only three weeks in the studio in two blocks, touring Japan and Australia in the interim, and were already performing *The Dark Side of the Moon* in their live set—the resultant album was immediate, simple, fresh, and chock full of well-structured and focused songs.

> It was rapid stuff. We sat in a room, wrote, recorded, like a production line. It's good to work under extreme constraints of time.

David Gilmour, quoted in *Pigs Might Fly: The Inside Story of Pink Floyd* (2007)

With large helpings of country, blues, and folk-rock, and no song longer than five minutes, *Obscured by Clouds* is an oddity in the Pink Floyd catalogue: most of the songs are an English art-rock band's twist on the West Coast music of Jackson Brown; The Eagles; and Crosby, Stills & Nash. By the time of the album's release, Pink Floyd were already in the studio recording its follow-up.

Remixed stereo and 5.1 versions of the entire album were released as part of *The Early Years 1965–1972* in November 2016.

'Obscured by Clouds'

David Gilmour: music, slide guitar, VCS 3 synthesiser
Roger Waters: music, bass, VCS 3 synthesiser
Richard Wright: VCS 3 synthesiser, Hammond organ
Nick Mason: drums, electronic drums

A pulsing, ominous instrumental, with massed layers of Wright's new VSC 3 synthesiser, guitar, and the carefully recreated sound of electronic drums on Mason's regular kit. As with 'Careful with That Axe, Eugene' and 'One of These Days', 'Obscured by Clouds' in an exercise in dynamics on a single chord—and very good it is, too.

First performed in November 1972 for the Roland Petit ballet in Marseille and throughout *The Dark Side of the Moon* tour in 1973.

'When You're In'

David Gilmour: music, guitars
Roger Waters: music, bass
Richard Wright: music, Hammond organ, piano
Nick Mason: music, drums

A simple full-band jam that is an extension of 'Obscured by Clouds'.

Performed, always accompanied by 'Obscured by Clouds', between November 1972 and November 1973. The arrangement of both tracks could last up to fifteen minutes, and an extended 'When You're In' included a furious guitar solo from David Gilmour.

'Burning Bridges'

David Gilmour: guitar, slide guitar, vocals
Richard Wright: music, Hammond organ, vocals
Roger Waters: lyrics, bass
Nick Mason: drums, percussion

'Burning Bridges' is a product of the rare writing pairing of Roger Waters and Richard Wright—only three songs in the entire Pink Floyd catalogue bear this writing credit.[6] While there is an unfinished feeling to many of the songs on *Obscured by Clouds,* this does allow us to hear the beautiful simplicity of songs such as 'Burning Bridges' without the studio trickery or layers of overdubs usually present on Pink Floyd's albums. The key-changes are pure Richard Wright, jazzy without being clever;

David Gilmour's slide guitar is delicate and understated. At only three and a half minutes, this song could easily be twice the length and never outstay its welcome.

No known live performances.

'The Gold It's in the...'

Roger Waters: lyrics, bass
David Gilmour: music, vocals, guitars
Nick Mason: drums, percussion

Released as the B-side to 'Free Four' in Italy and Germany in 1972.

Working to a tight deadline, some of Pink Floyd's songs on *Obscured by Clouds* seem curiously unfinished. 'The Gold It's in the...' is a straightforward rocker about living life to the full, not so far from the West Coast songs of The Eagles or The Steve Miller Band. There are no keyboards, just uncharacteristically shallow lyrics.

> Come on, my friends / Let's make for the hills / They say there's gold but I'm looking for thrills.

No known live performances.

'Wot's... Uh the Deal?'

David Gilmour: music, guitars, lap steel guitar, vocals
Richard Wright: piano, Hammond organ
Roger Waters: lyrics, bass
Nick Mason: drums

The flip-side of the West Coast music scene—no lumpen rockers here, this is pure Crosby, Stills & Nash (Graham Nash is a long-time pal of David Gilmour), with a light country touch and a short, expressive lap steel guitar solo.

> The perfect synthesis of Waters' lyrical introspection and Gilmour's musical aspirations. For the next five years this uniquely creative balance would produce some of the greatest rock music ever heard.
>
> Cliff Jones, *Echoes* (1996)

No known live performances by Pink Floyd, but this song was performed by David Gilmour on his *On An Island* tour in 2006.

'Mudmen'

David Gilmour: music, guitar, slide guitar
Richard Wright: music, piano, Hammond organ, VCS 3 synthesiser, vibraphone, electric piano
Roger Waters: bass
Nick Mason: drums

A simple guitar-led expansion of the middle section of 'Burning Bridges', sounding a lot like passages from *The Dark Side of the Moon* in places, especially Gilmour's solo in 'Money'. Filler, yes, but of the highest pedigree.

No known live performances.

'Childhood's End'

David Gilmour: lyrics, music, guitars, vocals
Roger Waters: bass
Richard Wright: Hammond organ, VCS 3 synthesiser, Farfisa organ
Nick Mason: drums

Mid-paced and ominous, Gilmour's 'Childhood's End' was inspired by the 1953 science-fiction novella of the same name by Arthur C. Clarke, as was 'Watcher of the Skies' by Genesis, released a few months later.

'Childhood's End' was first performed at the Centre Sportif de l'Ile des Vannes, Saint-Ouen, France on 1 December 1972 (broadcast on the radio by RTL), and was played a few more times that month. It was also performed at a handful of shows in March 1973.

'Free Four'

Roger Waters: lyrics, music, vocals, bass
David Gilmour: guitars
Richard Wright: VCS3 synthesiser
Nick Mason: drums, tambourine

Released as a single in the US, Italy, and Germany in 1972.

'Free Four' might be 'a relaxed, radio-friendly, throwaway, chorus-less, three-chord country chugger' as Toby Manning writes, but it is filled with typical Roger Waters abrasion: 'Life is a short, warm moment / And death is a long cold rest'.[7]

Early examples of themes that would dominate later work are on show here: mortality, Waters' father's death, and the all-devouring music industry.

The song received considerable airplay in the US and was partially responsible for breaking the market ahead of the success of *The Dark Side of the Moon*.

No known live performances.

'Stay'

Richard Wright: music, vocals, piano
David Gilmour: guitar, vocals
Roger Waters: lyrics, bass
Nick Mason: drums

Released as the B-side to 'Free Four' in the US in 1972.

A lost Pink Floyd classic and one of Richard Wright's best songs, with poetic lyrics by Waters. 'Stay' is a slow-moving, emotional piano ballad, with Wright's ghostly vocals beefed up by a Gilmour harmony.

'Stay' also has strong echoes of 'Summer '68', not just in its lyrical message but also in the verse chords reused from Wright's song from *Atom Heart Mother*. It even literally looks back to 1968 by borrowing some chord changes from 'Remember a Day': 'Why can't we play today / Why can't we stay that way'.

No known live performances.

'Absolutely Curtains'

Richard Wright: music, Farfisa and Hammond organ, tack piano, Wurlitzer electric piano, VCS3 synthesiser
Nick Mason: music, percussion
Roger Waters: music
David Gilmour: music

Music from the closing moments of the film, written and performed by Rick Wright, but credited to the whole band. Wright's slow-moving elegy is performed on multi-layered Farfisa and Hammond organ, piano, Wurlitzer, and VCS3 synthesiser. It sounds, in places, like the opening moments of 'Shine on You Crazy Diamond'.

The last part of the track is a chant by the Mapuga tribe of New Guinea.

No known live performances.

Reviews

> The stately, ominous 'Childhood's End' and the jaunty pop tune 'Free Four', [are] two songs whose obsessions with life, death and the past clearly point toward *The Dark Side of the Moon*. These tunes, blended with the sensibility of *Meddle*, suggest what Pink Floyd was about to develop into.

Stephen Thomas Erlewine, *AllMusic*

> One of the lost treasures of classic rock and, by far, the most overlooked album in the Pink Floyd catalogue
>
> Ric Albano, *Classic Rock Review* (November 2012)

The Dark Side of the Moon (1973)

Recorded May–June 1972, October 1972, and January–February 1973 at EMI Studios, Abbey Road, London. Produced by Pink Floyd. First released 24 March 1973 (UK: Harvest SHVL 804); 10 March 1973 (US: Harvest SMAS 11153)

While arguably not their masterpiece, *The Dark Side of the Moon* is certainly Pink Floyd's most famous and best-selling album. Its unprecedented and enduring success changed everything for the four men in Pink Floyd. Collectively and individually, they have never been able to escape the long shadow it casts.

> Perhaps the closest I will get to immortality will be through *The Dark Side of the Moon.*
>
> David Gilmour, *Sunday Telegraph* (2006)

> I think with *Dark Side* we had sort of achieved what we'd set out to achieve as young men going into the music business and after that we kind of clung together out of fear more than out of hope, in my view.
>
> Roger Waters, Billboard.com (2006)

> You couldn't really have lived through the seventies and remained unaware of *The Dark Side of the Moon.*
>
> Mark Radcliffe, *Reelin' in the Years* (2011)

As in 1970 and 1971, the early weeks of 1972 for Pink Floyd were spent writing and rehearsing a new piece for live performance. Roger Waters' proposal was not for a side-length epic such as 'Atom Heart Mother' or 'Echoes', but for an album-length song cycle dealing with a single subject: the pressures of modern life. Waters would write all of the lyrics in a newer, direct style, and the music would be written by Waters, Gilmour, and Wright more or less equally.

> I can remember sitting in Nick Mason's kitchen explaining it to the rest of the band; that the whole record might be about the pressures and preoccupations that divert us from our potential for positive action.
>
> Roger Waters, *The Dark Side of the Moon: The Making of Pink Floyd's Masterpiece* (2005)

The work-in-progress was debuted at The Dome in Brighton on 20 January 1972. Technical problems meant the performance ended during 'Money', but the entire piece was successfully performed the following evening at Portsmouth Guildhall. At this stage, *The Dark Side of the Moon* consisted of sections called 'Breathe', 'The Travel Sequence', 'Time', 'Home Again', 'Religion', 'Money', 'Us and Them', 'Scat', and 'Lunatic'.

There would be many changes as the piece was polished before and after recording commenced at the end of May 1972. 'Speak to Me' would be added in the studio. 'The Travel Sequence' would be replaced with 'On the Run' during studio sessions. 'Home Again' was renamed 'Breathe' (reprise). 'Religion' (also sometimes called 'The Mortality Sequence') was initially played on organ and would be given the name 'The Great Gig in the Sky' when re-arranged for piano. 'Scat' would later be titled 'Any Colour You Like' and 'Lunatic' became 'Brain Damage'. 'Eclipse' (initially simply 'End') would be added to live performances in early February.

The band's tours of the UK (January–February 1972), Japan (March 1972), North America (April–May 1972) and Europe (May 1972) gave them the opportunity to make continual improvements to their performances.

Recording commenced at EMI Studios on 24 May 1972, and initial sessions lasted for four weeks. The band were assigned staff engineer Alan Parsons, who would become a major part of the recording process. 'Us and Them' was the first song to be recorded, followed by 'Money', 'Time', and 'The Great Gig in the Sky'.

A two-month break was followed by more concerts in Europe and North America (September–October 1972), before returning to EMI for a handful of recording sessions in mid–late October.

Following a European tour in November and December 1972, Pink Floyd returned to EMI on 9 January 1973 for another three weeks of sessions to complete work on the album. They recorded 'Brain Damage', 'Eclipse', 'Any Colour You Like' and 'On the Run', while fine-tuning the work they had already laid down in the previous sessions. Four female vocalists were hired to sing on three songs, and saxophonist Dick Parry was booked to play on 'Us and Them' and 'Money'. The voices and saxophones added a much-needed warmth and depth of sound to Pink Floyd's often clinical songs.

Clare Torry added her mesmerising vocal on 'The Great Gig in the Sky' on 21 January 1973. At around the same time, Waters devised a series of seemingly random questions—such as 'are you afraid of dying?'—and recorded the answers of anyone who happened to be at EMI that day. Snippets of the answers were woven into many songs on the album.

> The most interesting responses are from three questions. The first one was, 'When was the last time you were violent?' And when you'd answer that one, you'd move on to the next question, 'Where [*sic.*] you in the right?'. They just seemed to slide into the record without any kind of problem, they lived very comfortably with the music.
>
> Roger Waters interview, Billboard.com (May 2006)

As sessions wound to a close, and with Waters' and Gilmour's relationship showing strain, producer Chris Thomas was brought in to supervise and mediate the final mix.[8]

> When the record was finished I took a reel-to-reel copy home with me and I remember playing it for my wife then and I remember her bursting into tears when it was finished. And I thought, 'This has obviously struck a chord somewhere' and I was kind of pleased by that.
>
> Roger Waters interview, Billboard.com (May 2006)

Released in March 1973, *The Dark Side of the Moon* was Pink Floyd's first US No. 1 album, and would spend over 850 weeks in the Billboard chart.

'Speak to Me'

Nick Mason: composition, percussion, tape effects, tape loops
Roger Waters: tape effects, tape loops
Richard Wright: piano

As with 'Alan's Psychedelic Breakfast' from *Atom Heart Mother*, Nick Mason gets a writing credit for assembling sound effects: 'Speak to Me' was just about the last element added to *The Dark Side of the Moon*, but was based on a similar idea used in live performances over the previous year.

The ominous heartbeat introduction is particularly effecting, building tension that is only released as the tracks segues into 'Breathe'. The ticking clocks of 'Time', the cash register sounds of 'Money', the rumbling keyboards from 'On the Run', and the manic laughter of 'Brain Damage' act as an overture to the album as a whole.

'Breathe'

David Gilmour: music, guitars, pedal steel guitar, vocals
Roger Waters: lyrics, music, bass
Richard Wright: music, Hammond organ, electric piano
Nick Mason: drums, percussion

> A track so gentle, light and leisurely-paced that's the aural equivalent of floating through Kew Gardens on a helium-filled pillow.
>
> Richard Smirke, Billboard.com (16 March 2013)

The simplest of wide-open chord changes with a rich production and Gilmour's gorgeous lap-steel ushers in the first song proper on *The Dark Side of the Moon*.[9]

Parts of 'Breathe' were inspired by Rick Wright's love of Miles Davis.

> There's a certain chord [in 'Breathe'] that is totally down to a chord in heard in *Kind of Blue*. That chord I just loved.
>
> Richard Wright in *Making of The Dark Side of the Moon* (2003)

The opening lyric of 'Breathe' was borrowed from a song of the same name written by Waters for his 1970 collaboration with Ron Geesin.

'On the Run'

David Gilmour: music, guitar, EMS Synthi AKS
Roger Waters: music, VCS3 synthesiser
Richard Wright: music, Hammond organ
Nick Mason: percussion

During 1972, 'On the Run' (or 'The Travel Sequence' as it was then known), was a simple, seven-minute guitar and drum jam, and would remain so for the rest of that year's performances.[10] It was recorded as such in early sessions for *The Dark Side of the Moon,* [11] and would only take its familiar form only after being rerecorded from scratch in a new arrangement in January 1973.

> If you've heard one of those bootlegs, you might have heard a different version of it. We had a sort of guitar passage, but it wasn't very good. We'd just got this new synthesiser and in the lid there was a little sequencer thing. I was playing with the sequencer device attachment and came up with this sound, which is the basic sound of it.
>
> David Gilmour, *Shades of Pink* radio programme (1984)

> ...Agitated drums, pulsing synthesisers, the sound of feet running, fleeing.
>
> quoted from Jo Nesbø, *The Thirst* (Vintage Digital, 2017)

This new piece replaced the original jam late in the album's recording sessions. The endlessly repeating synthesiser motif, overlaid with the sounds of running footsteps, airport announcements, heavy breathing, and manic laughter, certainly gives the impression of ceaseless movement.

'Time' / 'Breathe (Reprise)'

David Gilmour: music, guitars, vocals
Richard Wright: music, Farfisa organ, Wurlitzer electric piano, VCS 3 synthesiser, vocals
Roger Waters: lyrics, music, bass
Nick Mason: drums, roto-toms
Doris Troy: backing vocals
Lesley Duncan: backing vocals
Liza Strike: backing vocals
Barry St. John: backing vocals

'Time' is introduced with a long passage of clocks chiming and alarms ringing, recorded as a test by Alan Parsons, not specifically for the album. This is followed by a lengthy, heavily reverbed drum passage and long drawn-out chords.

> The drums used on the 'Time' track are roto-toms. I think we did some experiments with some other drums called boo-bans, which are very small, tuned drums, but the roto-toms actually gave the best effect.
>
> Nick Mason, *Shades of Pink* radio programme (1984)

When the song finally gets going, it combines urgency and a gentle wistfulness in equal measures. The song is lifted by Waters' clever internal rhymes (around / ground / town), and Gilmour's slow, melodic, and aurally super-charged guitar solo.

> I know a guy who works in a clinic for drug addicts, alcoholics and child molesters. I met him in my local pub and he'd heard the song 'Time' where there's the phrase 'hanging on in quiet desperation'. That moved him a lot because it had a bearing on what he himself felt. That made me realise if I were to express my feelings, vague and disturbed as they are, as honesty as I could, then that's the most I can do.
>
> Roger Waters, *Street Life* (24 January 1976)

Waters' original demo can be heard in the documentary *The Making of The Dark Side of the Moon* (2003).

'Breathe (Reprise)' serves as a coda to 'Time', and is simply a third verse of the opening song, carefully arranged to join seamlessly with the previous track.

'The Great Gig in the Sky'

Richard Wright: music, piano, Hammond organ
David Gilmour: pedal steel guitar
Roger Waters: bass
Nick Mason: drums, percussion
Clare Torry: vocal composition and performance

> The greatest piece of music Erik Satie never wrote.
>
> Guy Pratt, *My Bass and Other Animals* (2007)

'The Great Gig in the Sky' is a Richard Wright chord progression, known as 'The Mortality Sequence' or 'Religion', first performed in 1972 as a simple organ instrumental with spoken-word samples from the Bible and snippets of Malcolm Muggeridge, a British writer known for his conservative religious views. It was re-arranged for piano and recorded on 25 June 1972. Feeling the song needed something else the band tried different sound effects including NASA astronauts communicating on space missions. Finally, as sessions were drawing to a close, 25-year-old songwriter and session singer Clare Torry recorded her stunning vocal contribution in three takes on 21 January 1973, one of the very last sessions for the album.

Torry's supreme, almost orgasmic, singing lit up the track, a rare glimpse of soul in an often all-too-clinical band.

> The end result was a dramatic, striking performance conjuring sex, fear, death: all the component parts of the album. For Clare, though, it had been just another studio session. She collected her £30 and was home in time for dinner.
>
> Mark Blake, *Pigs Might Fly: The Inside Story of Pink Floyd* (2007)

Mention should also be made of Gilmour's weeping pedal steel guitar during the opening minutes of the track—another unusual and distinctive addition to the band's sound palette.

In 2012, readers of Rolling Stone voted Torry's singing on this track as the second best vocal performance in rock history.[12]

In 2004, Torry sued Pink Floyd and EMI for songwriting royalties, arguing that her contribution constituted co-authorship; all releases after 2005 now credit her and Richard Wright as co-writers.

The live debut of 'The Great Gig in the Sky', then called 'Religion', was organ-based, with tapes of preachers reading from passages from the bible. From September 1972, the more familiar piano arrangement would be performed, but without vocals and with spoken extracts from Ephesians. This was sometimes called 'The Mortality Sequence'.

The song was also performed throughout the live tours of 1987—1990 and in 1994. Clare Torry's vocals were recreated by an array of different backing singers except once: Clare herself sang the song at Pink Floyd's Knebworth appearance on 30 June 1990.[13] 'The Great Gig in the Sky' was also performed by Pink Floyd at manager Steve O'Rourke's funeral in Chichester Cathedral in 2003.

'Money'

David Gilmour: vocals, guitars
Roger Waters: lyrics, music, bass
Richard Wright: electric piano
Nick Mason: drums
Dick Parry: tenor saxophone

The sound of ringing cash tills that open Pink Floyd's most commercially successful song shows hints of Roger Water's deeply ironic sense of humour. This very commercial song in an unorthodox 7/8 (or perhaps 7/4) time signature became a big hit when released as a single in the US. Pink Floyd's cash register was soon ringing for real. However, perhaps the biggest irony is that the song's protagonist, a slave to money, is part of a very English band's twisted version of the black man's blues.

> Roger wrote 'Money' from the heart.
>
> David Gilmour, *Melody Maker* (19 May 1973)

> Although it's based around a bass line, I wrote it on an acoustic guitar. Occasionally, I would do things and Dave would say, 'No, that's wrong. There should be another beat. That's only seven.' I'd say, 'Well, that's how it is.' A number of my songs have bars of odd length. That's how the demo was. There's a very bluesy feel to it.
>
> Roger Waters interviewed by John Harris, *Rolling Stone* (March 2003)

The opening sound effects were assembled by Roger Waters and later rerecorded during the album sessions.

> I made those recordings in a shed at the bottom of the garden, throwing coins into a big industrial bowl that my wife used for mixing clay.
>
> Roger Waters interviewed by John Harris, *Rolling Stone* (March 2003)

The heavily edited 7-inch single version—cut from 6:22 to 3:59—includes the following sections of the album track: 0:00–0:09, 0:12–0:19, 0:26–0:33, 0:40–2:15 (central section of saxophone solo removed), 2:41–3:42 (second and third sections of guitar solo removed), 5:05–end.[14]

'Money' was rerecorded for the 1981 compilation album *A Collection of Great Dance Songs*, where Gilmour plays every instrument except the saxophone.[15] It is a fair facsimile, even if Gilmour's drum patterns are much simplified in comparison to the original.

Waters' original demo has been released on the *Experience* and *Discovery* versions of *The Dark Side of the Moon*. An extract was broadcast by BBC Radio One on 28 July 1992, during an interview with David Gilmour.

'Us and Them'

David Gilmour: guitars, vocals
Richard Wright: music, Hammond organ, piano, vocals
Roger Waters: lyrics, bass
Nick Mason: drums
Dick Parry: tenor saxophone
Lesley Duncan: backing vocals
Doris Troy: backing vocals
Barry St. John: backing vocals
Liza Strike: backing vocals

Surely among the very best Pink Floyd songs of all, 'Us and Them' originated with a rejected submission to the *Zabriskie Point* soundtrack. Titled 'The Violent Sequence' or 'The Riot Scene', it was performed in concert a few times in 1970 and brought to the first recording session for *The Dark Side of the Moon,* where it formed the verse sections of 'Us and Them'. Richard Wright's piano-only demo—simple, egg-shell fragile, elegant, and quite beautiful—is available on both the *Immersion* box set of *The Dark Side of the Moon*, released in 2011, and on *The Early Years 1967–1972,* released in 2016.

As with sessions for *Atom Heart Mother* and *Meddle,* as well as the later *Wish You Were Here*, one wonders if Pink Floyd consciously started their latest projects with their strongest new material.

Waters' damning lyric has some of his best imagery:

> Forward he cried from the rear / And the front rank died / The generals sat / And the lines on the map / Moved from side to side.
>
> A lament for the fact that human conflict is so commonplace as to seem utterly mundane.
>
> John Harris, *The Dark Side of the Moon: The Making of Pink Floyd's Masterpiece* (2005)

Dick Parry's warm, breathy sax—rough mixes have three intertwining saxophone parts—also suit the moody, smoky nature of 'Us and Them'.

> Of the songs that Roger and I have written together I would say that ['Us and Them'] is my favourite.
>
> Richard Wright in *Making of The Dark Side of the Moon* (2003)

'Any Colour You Like'

David Gilmour: music, guitars, vocals
Richard Wright: music, Hammond organ, VCS 3 synthesiser, EMS Synthi A, Minimoog
Roger Waters: music, bass
Nick Mason: music, drums, percussion

Released as the B-side to 'Money' in the US.

A simple guitar-led jam originally called 'Scat', it rings the changes from 'Breathe'. Careful studio arrangement and a nifty production lifts this piece above its very simple structure.

> Colliding clouds of sublime Stratocaster.
>
> Mark Radcliffe, *Reelin' in the Years* (2011)

'Brain Damage'

Roger Waters: lyrics, music, bass, vocals
David Gilmour: guitars, vocals
Richard Wright: Hammond organ, VCS3 synthesiser
Nick Mason: drums, bells
Lesley Duncan: backing vocals
Doris Troy: backing vocals
Barry St. John: backing vocals
Liza Strike: backing vocals

Written during the final sessions for *Meddle* in summer 1971, this simple finger-picked song, a direct development of 'Grantchester Meadows' and 'If', closed the original live arrangement of *The Dark Side of the Moon*.

The lyrics invoke Syd Barrett, dealing directly with madness, and are almost overwhelmed by a lush production resplendent with vocal harmonies, female backing singers, and iridescent washes of Hammond organ.

> Syd had been the central creative force in the early days and so his having succumbed to schizophrenia was an enormous blow. And also, when you see that happening to someone you've been very close friends with and known more or less your

> whole life, it really concentrates the mind on how ephemeral one's sensibilities and mental capacities can be. For me, it was very much 'There but for the grace of God go I.'

Roger Waters interviewed by John Harris, *Rolling Stone* (March 2003)

'Eclipse'

Roger Waters: lyrics, music, bass, vocals
David Gilmour: guitars, vocals
Richard Wright: Hammond organ
Nick Mason: drums, percussion
Lesley Duncan: backing vocals
Doris Troy: backing vocals
Barry St. John: backing vocals
Liza Strike: backing vocals

> We performed it for some time without an ending. One day I suddenly said, 'Hey, guess what, I think I've written the ending.'

Roger Waters interview, Billboard.com (May 2006)

'Eclipse' is a repeating cycle of four descending chords, which succeed in adding a gloriously uplifting effect—amplified by Doris Troy's magnificent gospel backing vocals—to a lyric which is decidedly downbeat.

> And all that is now / And all that is gone / And all that's to come / And everything under the sun is in tune / But the sun is eclipsed by the moon.

> *The Dark Side of the Moon* finished off Pink Floyd once and for all. To be that successful is the aim of every group. And once you've cracked it, it's all over.

Roger Waters, interviewed by Chris Salewicz (June 1987)

Live Performances

'Speak to Me', 'Breathe', 'The Travel Sequence', 'Time', 'Breathe (Reprise)', 'Religion' and an abruptly truncated 'Money' were first performed at the Brighton Dome on 20 January 1972. 'Us and Them', 'Any Colour You Like', and 'Brain Damage' were first performed the next night at the Portsmouth Guildhall (although 'The Violent Sequence' was performed in concert a handful of times during the first half of 1970). The live debut of 'Eclipse' was at the Colston Hall, Bristol, on 5 February 1972.[16] The full album would remain in the band's set list at every concert played in 1972: live recordings of 'The Travel Sequence', 'Religion', and 'Any Colour You Like' (recorded in Brighton on 29 June 197), are available on the *Immersion* box set of *The Dark Side of the Moon*, released in 2011.

The more familiar arrangements 'On the Run' and 'The Great Gig in the Sky' would debut in Madison, WA, on 4 March 1973, on the first date of their post-album release US tour. The full album would remain in the band's set list at every concert played through 1973–1975. A live version of the entire album, recorded on 16 November 1974, is available on the *Immersion* box set of *The Dark Side of the Moon*.

'Us and Them' and 'Money' were performed as encores during the *In the Flesh* tour between January–July 1977.

'On the Run', 'Time' (without 'Breathe (Reprise)'), 'The Great Gig in the Sky', 'Money', and 'Us and Them' were included in all full shows in the *Momentary Lapse of Reason* tour between 1987 and 1989. Live versions of these songs, recorded at Nassau Coliseum between 19–23 August 1988, are available on *Delicate Sound of Thunder* (out 22 November 1988).

'Time', 'Breathe (Reprise)', 'The Great Gig in the Sky, 'Money', and 'Us and Them' were included in every show during the *The Division Bell* tour in 1994. The complete *Dark Side of the Moon* album was performed in full on occasion on the same tour, and a cut-and-paste live version of the entire album is available on *P•U•L•S•E* (released 29 May 1995). The recording dates on *P•U•L•S•E* were:

'Speak to Me', Rome, 20 September 1994;
'Breathe', London, 20 October 1994;
'On the Run', London, 20 October 1994;
'Time' and 'Breathe (Reprise)', edited from performances in Modena (17 September 1994), Rome (20 September 1994), and London (20 October 1994);
'The Great Gig in the Sky', London, 20 October 1994;
'Money', edited from performances in Modena (17 September 1994) and London (20 October 1994);
'Us and Them', edited from performances in London on 19 and 20 October 1994;
'Any Colour You Like', edited from performances in London on 19 and 23 October 1994;
'Brain Damage', London, 19 October 1994;
'Eclipse', London, 19 October 1994.

'The Great Gig in the Sky' was performed by Pink Floyd at manager Steve O'Rourke's funeral in Chichester Cathedral in 2003. 'Speak to Me', 'Breathe', 'Breathe (Reprise)', and 'Money' also formed part of the set by the reunited Pink Floyd at Live 8 on 2 July 2005.

Review

> If it is not exactly the most feel-good party record you've ever heard, it works perfectly on its own terms, ends superbly, and, with 10 tracks on it, is positively sprightly when you compare it with some of their other work, whose length, you feel, was constrained only by the limited amount of vinyl on one side of an album.
>
> Nicholas Lezard, *The Guardian*, 9 April 2013

Wish You Were Here (1975)

Recorded January–July 1975 at EMI Studios, Abbey Road, London. Produced by Pink Floyd. First released 12 September 1975 (UK: Harvest SHVL 814; US: CBS CK 33453).

In many ways, *Wish You Were Here* is Pink Floyd's 'difficult second album'. The global success of *The Dark Side of the Moon* effectively kickstarted the third phase of Pink Floyd. The Barrett years of 1967–1968 and the 'art rock' years through to 1972 would now transform to an odd kind of global stardom, where the band name sold millions of records but the individual members remained curiously anonymous.

Whereas *The Dark Side of the Moon* had touched on the themes of loss and mental illness, the follow-up, *Wish You Were Here*, is an album about the negative aspects of Floyd's new-found fame—either the dissatisfaction of being a small cog in the heartless music industry ('Welcome to the Machine', 'Have a Cigar') or eulogies for the loss of Syd Barrett, who never recovered from the band's initial success ('Shine on You Crazy Diamond', 'Wish You Were Here'). Roger Waters' increasing dissatisfaction in the trappings of fame would reach its apogee, of course, in Pink Floyd's dystopian concept album *The Wall* (1979).

Having toured *The Dark Side of the Moon* through Europe and North America in 1973, Pink Floyd returned to the recording studio in October that year to commence their next project: a follow-up to their most successful album to date.

The sessions resulted in an extended false start—the revisiting of an idea to record an album without any familiar musical instruments whatsoever.[17]

> There was an abortive attempt to make an album not using any musical instruments. It seemed like a good idea at the time, but it didn't come together. Probably because we needed to stop for a bit.
>
> From Roger Waters' interview with Nick Sedgewick in *A Rambling Conversation with Roger Waters Concerning All This and That* (1985)

> I remember sitting down with Roger and saying, 'Roger, this is insane!'
>
> Richard Wright in *Which One's Pink?* (2007)

Two tracks from this project were made available in 2011: 'The Hard Way', a basic rhythm track of footsteps and rubber bands; and 'Wine Glasses', which was later incorporated into the opening chords of 'Shine on You Crazy Diamond'.[18]

Pink Floyd returned to live performances in June 1974 with a seven-date tour of France. Always keen to debut new material, these concerts marked the first live performances of two new pieces: 'Shine On' and 'Raving and Drooling', which had been worked up in the preceding weeks at Kingsway rehearsal studios in London. By November 1974 and a lengthy UK tour, a third piece had been added, at this stage titled, 'You've Got to Be Crazy'. When the four band members entered EMI Studios in Abbey Road in January 1975, the expectation was that these three songs would be recorded for their new album.

After some weeks of minimal progress, Waters suggested another idea. With 'Shine On' as the centrepiece of the album, already written as a eulogy to Syd Barrett and his mental destruction by the music business, Waters suggested expanding this concept through two new songs comprising thinly veiled attacks on the business itself. The lyrics of 'Have a Cigar' and 'Welcome to the Machine' worked with 'Shine On' to provide an apt summary of the rise and fall of Barrett.

> At the start it was entirely about Syd. It's a sad piece and a deep moan.
>
> Nick Mason, interviewed in *Ciao 2001* (May 1975)

> 'Shine On' is not really about Syd—he's just a symbol for all the extremes of absence some people have to indulge in because it's the only way they can cope with how fucking sad it is, modern life, to withdraw completely. I found that terribly sad.
>
> Roger Waters quoted in *Crazy Diamond: Syd Barrett & the Dawn of Pink Floyd* (2001) by Mike Watkinson and Pete Anderson

'Raving and Drooling' and 'You've Got to Be Crazy' had no place in this concept and were set aside, for now at least.[19]

Returning to the studio and May and June, with the title track written and recorded mid-way through the sessions, Pink Floyd completed their ninth studio album that July. A release date was set for 12 September 1975.

'Shine On You Crazy Diamond, Parts I to VI'

Roger Waters: lyrics, music, bass, vocals, glass harp
David Gilmour: music, guitars, vocals, EMS Synthi AKS, glass harp
Richard Wright: music, Hammond organ, ARP String Ensemble, Minimoog, VCS 3 synthesiser, clavinet, piano, glass harp, vocals
Nick Mason: drums, percussion

Dick Parry: baritone and tenor saxophones
Carlena Williams: backing vocals
Venetta Fields: backing vocals

Initially laid down as a single twenty-five-minute piece, recording this classic song took up most of the initial sessions for the album.[20] Its composition started with a simple four-note guitar phrase, which became known as 'Syd's Theme'. From here, Waters, Wright and Gilmour co-composed the various phases of the music, and, as usual, Waters wrote the lyrics which simultaneously mourn and celebrate Syd.

> 'Shine On You Crazy Diamond' was written with odd little musical ideas coming out of various people. The main phrase came from Dave and we worked from there until we had the various parts of 'Shine On' finished.
>
> Roger Waters, interviewed in October 1975 by Nick Sedgewick

> First of all we did a basic track from the beginning where the first guitar solo starts, right through 'Shine On' and the part with the sax solo through to the continuation of 'Shine On'. That was in all twenty minutes (sic) long, which was at one time going to be the whole of one side of the album.
>
> David Gilmour, interview with Gary Cooper from the *Wish You Were Here* songbook.

> Arguably the Floyd's finest single achievement since Syd Barrett's departure into schizophrenic exile nearly seven years earlier.
>
> Cliff Jones, *Echoes* (1996)

Recording sessions for 'Shine On' were not without their problems and challenges, however. Firstly, the entire backing track had to be rerecorded:

> We originally did the backing track over the course of several days, but we came to the conclusion that it just wasn't good enough. So we did it again in one day flat and got it a lot better. Unfortunately nobody understood the desk properly and when we played it back we found that someone had switched the echo returns from monitors to tracks one and two. That affected the tom-toms and guitars and keyboards which were playing along at the time. There was no way of saving it, so we just had to do it yet again.
>
> David Gilmour, interview with Gary Cooper from *Wish You Were Here* songbook

After this, during later sessions in either June or July (sources vary but the strongest evidence suggests 5 June), the band had a mysterious visitor.

> Roger was there and he was sitting at the desk and I came in and I saw this guy sitting behind him—a huge, bald, fat guy. I thought, 'He looks a bit strange' Anyway, so I sat down with Roger at the desk and we worked for about ten minutes and this guy kept on getting up and brushing his teeth and then sitting—doing really weird things, but keeping quiet. And I said to Roger, 'Who is he?' and Roger said 'I don't know.' and I said 'Well, I assumed he was a friend of yours,' and he said 'No, I don't know who he is.' Anyway, it took me a long time and then suddenly I realised it was Syd.
>
> Richard Wright (1984).[21]

Barrett, by now deep into withdrawal, made some comments about the recording and slipped away later in the day. Allegedly, none of the band members ever saw him again.

When 'Shine On' was cut in two later in the sessions, this first section consisted of five parts.:

Part I (0:00–3:54) has dawn-of-time synthesisers and wine glasses with a bluesy guitar solo
Part II (3:54–6:27) begins with Gilmour's four-note 'Syd's Theme' and runs through a slow guitar solo
Part III (6:27–8:42) starts with Wright's minimoog solo and includes a third, more aggressive guitar solo from Gilmour
Part IV (8:42–11:10) Waters sings the verses, with Gilmour, Wright and the Blackberries on harmonies.
Part V (11:10–13:32) saxophone solos, played by Dick Parry. A machine-like hum segues into 'Welcome to the Machine'.

Intriguingly, when this song was remixed in 5.1 for the SA CD (released in 2011), it included a new piano overdub by Richard Wright.

> In mixing 'Shine On You Crazy Diamond parts I through V', I noticed that there was a missing piano part. After the second guitar solo there's a verse section where Rick plays a horn solo on the Minimoog and on the original stereo mix of the album there is an acoustic piano part behind that solo blocking the chord changes. It was nowhere to be found on the multi-tracks. I began to speculate about what may have happened. [I concluded that] they were at Abbey Road doing a playback of the completed mix and somebody may have said 'I think we should have had piano in that verse behind the minimoog solo' and somebody else may have said 'well, we're certainly not going to remix it'. So a logical solution would have been to play the [finished] mix back and have Rick play a live piano overdub to the master mix. It does mean that the piano part would only exist on that master tape and not on the multi-track. I phoned Rick and said 'Why don't you come down to the studio and we can have a go at overdubbing that piano?' Rick came down that evening and we listened very carefully

> to the original and tried to match as closely as we possibly could what he had played more than thirty years earlier.
>
> James Guthrie, quoted in *The Missing Piano* short film (2012)

Wright died in September 2008, so one assumes that this overdub was his last ever recording session.

Official Edits of the Original Studio Tracks

A Collection of Great Dance Songs, edited to 10:33 comprising Parts I, II, IV and VII.

Echoes, edited to 17:32 and comprising Parts I, II, III, IV, V, VI, and VII—the only official release of Parts V and VI running together.

A Foot in the Door, edited to 11:03 and comprising Parts I (with 80 seconds removed), II, III (with 69 seconds removed), IV, and V.

Other promo edits (e.g., for the *Shine On* sampler) either fade in late or fade out early.

An edited version of Part I was issued in France and Italy as the B-side to the 'Have a Cigar' single (15 November 1975). This simply fades at 3:53.

'Welcome to the Machine'

David Gilmour: guitars, vocals
Nick Mason: timpani, cymbals
Roger Waters: lyrics, music, bass, VCS 3 synthesiser
Richard Wright: VCS 3 synthesiser, Hammond organ, ARP String synthesiser, Minimoog

As Mark Blake writes in *Pigs Might Fly*, 'Welcome to the Machine' is 'a bleak dissertation on the human condition and those who spent their lives in search of a dream, only to find that the machine runs on dreams and very little else'.

Waters' lyrics examine his increasing disillusionment with the music industry. With echoes of George Orwell's dystopian *1984*, where every moment and every decision is controlled, 'Welcome to the Machine' hints at Waters' frustration that the demands of the music industry ('the machine') are repressing his personal identity and artistic expression.

Dominated by Wright's throbbing VSC3 synthesiser, 'Welcome to the Machine' is almost interminably desolate in its message and music. It does sound great on headphones, though.[22]

The lead vocal is by David Gilmour.

> The only time we've ever used tape speed to help us with vocals was on one line of The Machine Song. It was a line I just couldn't reach so we dropped the tape down half a semitone and then dropped the line in on the track.
>
> David Gilmour, *Wish You Were Here* songbook

'Have a Cigar'

Roger Waters: lyrics, music, bass
David Gilmour: guitars, keyboards
Richard Wright: electric piano, ARP String Synthesiser, Minimoog, Hohner clavinet
Nick Mason: drums
Roy Harper: vocals

'Have a Cigar' takes syncopated bass, guitar, and clavinet in a harder rock sound than the rest of the album, and marries them to a scathing critique of the hypocrisy of the music business. Lead vocals are by the British songwriter Roy Harper, who was recording his own album at Abbey Road concurrently, and was invited to sing after both Gilmour and Waters failed to achieve a suitable take.[23]

Despite his own considerable artistic success, 'Have a Cigar' has become Harper's most celebrated performance.

> Everyone thought it was Roger. I was a bit peed off about that.
>
> Roy Harper quoted in *Pink Floyd: The Story of Wish You Were Here*

Waters, however, believes that he could have done a better job himself.

> I think if I'd persevered with it, I would have done it better. I think if I'd have sung it, it would have been more vulnerable and less cynical than the way he did it.
>
> Quoted in *Pink Floyd: The Story of Wish You Were Here*

After an unusually aggressive Gilmour guitar solo, hinting at his work on *Animals* the following year, the song ends with a clever audio effect.

> We made a copy of the mix and ran it through eq. to make it very middly, knocking out all the bass and most of the high top so that it sounds radio-like. The interference was recorded on my car cassette radio and all we did was to put that track on top of the original track.
>
> David Gilmour, *Wish You Were Here* songbook

'Have a Cigar' was issued as a single in some territories; the single edit fades 40 seconds before the end of the album version.

> 'Have a Cigar' isn't cynicism, it's sarcasm. In fact, it's not even sarcasm, it's realism.
>
> Roger Waters, *Street Life* (24 January 1976)

'Wish You Were Here'

David Gilmour: music, guitars, pedal steel guitar, vocals
Nick Mason: drums
Roger Waters: music, lyrics, bass
Richard Wright: piano, Minimoog
Stéphane Grappelli: violin

Pink Floyd had often performed short and reflective folky acoustic songs, both in their live sets and their albums. Songs such as 'Julia Dream', 'Crying Song', 'Cymbaline', 'Grantchester Meadows', 'If', 'Fat Old Sun', and 'A Pillow of Winds' provided welcome contrast to the lengthy spaced-out electric jams that dominated the post-Barrett output.

'Wish You Were Here', a stately ballad with a hint of country, is perhaps their most celebrated acoustic song. Segueing from 'Have a Cigar' with radio effects that suggest the listener is switching channels, the opening chords are played on a heavily processed twelve-string acoustic guitar, with a second acoustic providing the lead melody, mixed away from centre to suggest that the guitarist is playing along with the radio. Gilmour's pedal steel guitar, a key component of country music, plays an important role in the instrumentation, as does Wright's sparse piano counterpoint.

The lyrics are a study in detachment: that there is something missing in everything. Waters dedicated the Live 8 performance to 'anyone who's not here. Particularly, of course, for Syd'.

An alternative take of 'Wish You Were Here', featuring a violin solo by the French jazz violinist Stéphane Grappelli (1908–1997) was included in the 2011 *'Experience'* and *'Immersion'* re-releases of *Wish You Were Here*.

> 'Wish You Were Here' happened in the studio when was plonking that riff on the 12-string. I [first] played in the control room of Studio 3 at Abbey Road. It was just something I'd been strumming at home and Roger immediately said 'What's that?' We immediately worked it up and wrote the rest of the music.
>
> David Gilmour, interviewed for *The Pink Floyd and Syd Barrett Story* (2001)

Perhaps unexpectedly, 'Wish You Were Here' was recorded in an up-tempo arrangement by Wyclef Jean for his album *The Ecleftic: 2 Sides II a Book*. This version was released as a single in December 2001, peaking at #28 in the UK. The song was also performed at the closing ceremony of the London 2012 Olympics; sung by Ed Sheeran and performed by Richard Jones (of The Feeling), Mike Rutherford (of Genesis), and Nick Mason, their version entered the UK singles chart at #34 the following week. The Pink Floyd original simultaneously entered at #68, marking the first time it had entered the UK Top 75.

'Shine on You Crazy Diamond Parts VI to IX'

Roger Waters: music (parts VI–VIII), lyrics, bass, vocals, guitar
David Gilmour: music (parts VI–VIII), guitars, vocals, lap steel guitar, bass, EMS Synthi AKS
Richard Wright: music (all parts), Hammond organ, ARP String Ensemble, Minimoog, VCS 3 synthesiser, clavinet, Wurlitzer electric piano, Steinway piano, backing vocals
Nick Mason: drums, percussion
Carlena Williams: backing vocals
Venetta Fields: backing vocals

The second half of Floyd's classic anthem to Syd. A cross-fade from 'Wish You Were Here' is achieved with some wind effects and judicious mixing—the original recording has an insistent drum beat from the saxophone solo in Part V through to the introduction of the full band in Part VI.

> Part VI (0:00–4:39) begins with the wind effects from 'Wish You Were Here', as the music builds dynamically to a thrilling lap steel guitar solo by Gilmour
>
> Part VII (4:39–6:09) reprise of the vocal section: the third verse
>
> Part VIII (6:09–9:07) funky instrumental section. Bootleg recordings of the sessions reveal that part VIII was originally much longer—over eight minutes—and that the track faded after this section.
>
> Part IX (9:07–12:28) is a measured, keyboard-led coda

Perhaps less celebrated than Parts I to V, simply because it was never played live by the band after 1977, it is easy to overlook the skill, dynamics, and emotion of the musicianship in this second section of 'Shine on You Crazy Diamond'.[24]

Live Performances

Then called simply 'Shine On', 'Shine on You Crazy Diamond' was first performed on Pink Floyd's French and UK tours of 1974. This was very much a work in progress at this stage, with parts I and IX not yet included. A live version of this arrangement from 16 November 1974 is available on the *Immersion* box set of *Wish You Were Here*. Parts I to V and parts VI to IX (separated by 'Have a Cigar') were performed throughout the 1975 North American tour, and also at the band's Knebworth concert on 5 July 1975.

'Have a Cigar' was given its live debut in Vancouver on 8 April 1975, the first date of a lengthy two-part North American tour. Roy Harper joined the band to sing 'Have a Cigar' at the Knebworth concert.

All of the songs on *Wish You Were Here* were performed at all fifty-five dates of the 1977 *In the Flesh* tour, with 'Welcome to the Machine' and 'Wish You Were Here' receiving their live debuts on the first night of the tour at Westfalenhallen, Dortmund, West Germany on 23 January 1977.

'Welcome to the Machine' and 'Shine on You Crazy Diamond (Parts I–V)' were also performed at most dates of the 1987–1989 world tour; 'Wish You Were Here' at all of them. Live versions of the latter two songs that were recorded at Nassau Coliseum between 19–23 August 1988 are available on *Delicate Sound of Thunder*.

A shortened arrangement of 'Shine on You Crazy Diamond' (without Gilmour's solo in Part III) would open the second half of the shows on the group's 1994 *The Division Bell* tour, except on shows where all of *The Dark Side of the Moon* was performed—at these gigs, 'Shine on You Crazy Diamond' opened the first half of the show. For the last six weeks of this tour, the band added Part VII to Parts I, II, IV and V. A live version of this arrangement, plus the ever-constant 'Wish You Were Here', recorded at Earl's Court, London on 19 and 20 October 1994, are available on *P•U•L•S•E*.

Most memorably, the reunited Pink Floyd played 'Wish You Were Here' at Live 8 on 2 July 2005, with Gilmour and Waters trading verses for the first and last time.

Other Contemporary Songs

'The Merry Xmas Song'

A humorous song from around 1975, it is notable as the last of only five Pink Floyd songs to feature Nick Mason on vocals (the others are 'Scream Thy Last Scream', 'Corporal Clegg', 'One of These Days' and 'Signs of Life'). If you have not heard this, then you have not missed anything.

Reviews

> 'Shine on You Crazy Diamond' is initially credible because it purports to confront the subject of Syd Barrett, the long and probably forever lost guiding light of the original Floyd. But the potential of the idea goes unrealised; they give such a matter-of-fact reading of the goddamn thing that they might as well be singing about Roger Waters' brother-in-law getting a parking ticket.
>
> Ben Edmunds, *Rolling Stone* (6 November 1975)

> No dumb tribulations-of-a-rock-star epic here—the dedication to long-departed crazy Syd Barrett gives it an emotional resolve that mitigates what little self-pity lyricist Roger Waters allows himself. Even more remarkable, the music is not only simple and attractive, with the synthesiser used mostly for texture and the guitar breaks for comment, but it actually achieves some of the symphonic dignity (and cross-referencing) that *The Dark Side of the Moon* simulated so ponderously.
>
> Robert Christgau, *Village Voice* (1975)

Wish You Were Here must be my own Record of the Year, closely pursued by *Zuma, The Hissing of Summer Lawns,* Little Feat's *Last Record Album,* Dylan's *Blood on the Tracks* and Tangerine Dream's *Ricochet.*

John Peel, *The Listener* (January 1976)

4

Floyd Phase 4: 1976–1985 Nothing is Very Much Fun Any More

Animals (1977)

Recorded April–December 1976 at Britannia Row Studios, London. Produced by Pink Floyd. First released 23 January 1977 (UK: Harvest SHVL 815); 10 February 1977 (US: JC 34474).

Pink Floyd started work on their tenth studio album in April 1976, only six months after the release of *Wish You Were Here,* at their newly opened recording studio, Britannia Row. The studio was based in a converted church hall in Islington, North London. *Animals* marks the start of the period in the band's history that would be dominated by the work and vision of George Roger Waters.

All of the forthright *Animals* album would be recorded at Britannia Row, and work on the album would take up the rest of 1976.[1] Two songs originally performed live in 1974 and 1975 would be revisited for *Animals*: 'You've Got to Be Crazy' would be reworked into 'Dogs', and 'Raving and Drooling' became 'Sheep'. 'Pigs (Three Different Ones)' was a new Waters song; the two-part acoustic 'Pigs on the Wing' was a very late addition to the running order.

Much has been written saying that the aggression throughout *Animals* was Pink Floyd's reaction to the punk movement in the UK. While nihilism in the face of dystopia may have informed 'Pigs (Three Different Ones)', it is documented that over half of the album was written in 1974. The arrangements, though, are certainly less lush: there are no saxophone solos or female backing vocals to leaven the bleak messages herein.

> Of the old guard who were supposedly under threat, the so-called 'dinosaur' acts like Pink Floyd, most survived and even became more successful.
>
> Paul Du Noyer, *In the City* (2009)

> The first missive in a miserable trilogy.
>
> Toby Manning, *The Rough Guide to Pink Floyd* (2006)

When performing the album throughout 1977, the running order was changed to 'Sheep', 'Pigs on the Wing 1', 'Dogs', 'Pigs on the Wing 2', and 'Pigs (Three Different Ones)'.

'Pigs on the Wing (Part 1)'

Roger Waters: lyrics, music, guitar, vocals

A rarity in the Pink Floyd catalogue: a love song of sorts, and a fragile song of hope, with just one verse of acoustic guitar and vocals.

'Dogs'

David Gilmour: music, vocals, guitars
Roger Waters: lyrics, vocals, bass
Richard Wright: electric piano, Hammond organ, Minimoog, ARP String Ensemble, Farfisa organ, vocals
Nick Mason: drums, percussion

> 'Dogs' dispenses bite after venomous bite into the desires that drive us to seize the fast buck and screw anyone that gets in our way.
>
> James P. Wisdom, *Pitchfork* (2000)

One of the great unheralded Pink Floyd songs on this album—the other is 'Sheep'—'Dogs' starts with a deceptive acoustic jazz/folk strum, before building to a full-on rock song with a vividly bitter Waters lyric, its impact heightened by David Gilmour's rich, soulful vocal delivery.

'Dogs' focuses on the aggressive, competitive world of big business. The first two verses detail a businessman's predatory nature—outwardly charming and respectable, but willing to stab those who trust him in the back. Subsequent verses portray the emptiness of his existence.

Gilmour treats us to two of his very best guitar solos (1:46–2:29 and 5:32–6:48): emotional, biting, and vibrant, they fit this song absolutely perfectly. The song ends with a yowl of feedback.

'Pigs (Three Different Ones)'

Roger Waters: lyrics, music, vocals, guitar
David Gilmour: guitar, bass
Richard Wright: Hammond organ, ARP String Synthesiser, grand piano, clavinet
Nick Mason: drums, cowbell

'Pigs (Three Different Ones)' is the most aggressive song on the album and is not an easy listen. A variation on Pink Floyd's 'funky' style—see parts of 'Echoes' and 'Atom Heart Mother'—the song is powered by electric guitars and Gilmour's expressive bass-playing, not so far away from the churning arrangement of 'Have a Cigar'. A repetitive cowbell insistently holds the beat, while Rick Wright's contribution is not much more than muted piano in the left stereo channel.

Waters' lyrics are particularly vicious, actually calling out British morality campaigner Mary Whitehouse.

> I was incensed by Mary Whitehouse, as I am by all book-burners and bible-pushers; people who foster that sexual guilt and shame, who try and deny people any opportunity to fulfil their sexual destiny.
>
> Roger Waters interviewed by John Harris, *Mojo* (November 2004)

The song was performed at all fifty-five dates of the *In the Flesh* tour between January and July 1977. In concert, 'Pigs (Three Different Ones)' was a much harder beast, sometimes stretching to seventeen minutes or more. When this song was performed in Montreal in July 1977, a fan angered Waters by throwing a beer bottle onto the stage; Waters later called the fan to the stage and spat in his face. This incident has been cited as a catalyst for Pink Floyd's next album, *The Wall*.

'Sheep'

Roger Waters: lyrics, music, vocals, guitar
David Gilmour: guitar, bass, ARP Quadra synthesiser
Richard Wright: electric piano, Hammond organ, ARP String Synthesiser, Minimoog
Nick Mason: drums

Richard Wright's presence on *Animals* is much reduced, but his Fender Rhodes piano intro is perfect Pink Floyd, building a tension throughout the opening minutes of this compelling track. Meanwhile, Gilmour's stabbing guitar phrases and Waters' dramatic lyrics dominate.

Dating back as far as late 1973, 'Sheep', originally called 'Raving and Drooling', was the opening number for all of Pink Floyd's concerts from 1974–1977. Its climatic finale of tumbling guitar chords is pure Gilmour—clinical, powerfully aggressive, wholly in control.

'Sheep' echoes a number of earlier songs: we hear the same bubbling bass riff as 'One of These Days', the same octave-spanning bass guitar as 'Careful with That Axe, Eugene', and the same rising synth chord pattern as 'Welcome to the Machine'.

'Pigs on the Wing (Part 2)'

Roger Waters: lyrics, music, guitar, vocals

The second verse of Waters' acoustic love song to his wife Carolyne.[2]

'Pigs on the Wing' (8-track version)

Roger Waters: lyrics, music, acoustic guitar, vocals
Richard Wright: keyboards
Snowy White: electric guitar

A rather lovely hybrid of both parts of 'Pigs on the Wing', with a superbly melodic guitar solo bridging parts 1 and 2. The solo was played by Snowy White.

> I went into the studio to meet the band. And Roger had just said, 'I've got this new song, I'm going to do it like an acoustic guitar and stuff, but I want to do it quickly.' They were mixing the album and they wanted to put this little track on. So, he turned to me and said, 'Well as long as you're here, you might as well play on this one.' So I just picked up one of Dave's guitars and stuck a little bit in the middle of it.
>
> Snowy White, interviewed by Michael Simone for *REG* (2000)

Live Performances

'Raving and Drooling' was first performed in June 1974, with 'You've Got to Be Crazy' in November that year. Both songs were played at all subsequent live dates in 1974 and 1975. Live versions of these songs from 16 November 1974 are available on the *Immersion* box set of *Wish You Were Here* (7 November 2011).

All of the songs on *Animals* were performed at all fifty-five dates of the *In the Flesh* tour between January and July 1977, and none of them since by the full band.

Reviews

> Where Floyd's two most recognizable albums made their mark with operatic aggression and fear, *Animals* deals in dirt-under-the-fingernails reality, the common smallness that simultaneously binds and repels us all.
>
> James P. Wisdom, *Pitchfork* (2000)

> Like all Floyd records, this one absorbs like a sponge, but you can still hear the gooey screams of listeners who put up a fight. What's the problem? For starters, the sax

> that warmed *The Dark Side of the Moon* and *Wish You Were Here* has been replaced by a succession of David Gilmour guitar solos—thin, brittle and a sorry substitute indeed. The singing is more wooden than ever. The sound is more complex, but it lacks real depth; there's nothing to match the incredible intro to *The Dark Side of the Moon*. Somehow you get the impression that this band is being metamorphosed into a noodle factory.
>
> Frank Rose, *Rolling Stone* (March 1977)

> Pink Floyd's rare gift is to be at its most commercial when it is being most true to its obscure, menacing, surrealistic vision.
>
> *Billboard* (1977)

> Lyrical, ugly and rousing, all in the right places.
>
> Robert Christgau, *Christgau's Record Guide* (1981)

The Wall (1979)

Pre-production at Britannia Row, London (October 1978–March 1979). Album recorded at Super Bear Studio, Alpes Maritimes, France (April–July 1979); Studio Miraval, Correns, France (June–July 1979); Cherokee Recording Studios, Hollywood (September 1979); the Producers Workshop, Los Angeles (September–November 1979). Orchestra recorded at CBS 30th Street Studio, New York (Summer 1979). Produced by Roger Waters, David Gilmour, Bob Ezrin, and James Guthrie. First released 23 November 1979 (UK: Harvest SHDW 411); 8 January 1980 (US: Columbia PC2 36183)

6 July 1977. Olympic Stadium, Montreal. Roger Waters spits at a fan and the concept for Pink Floyd's next project is born. A huge seller, with over 10 million sales in the US alone, *The Wall* is, for want of a better term, a rock opera—that is, a series of interconnected songs conveying a complete story arc. Almost entirely written by Waters, the album follows Pink, a character modelled on Syd Barrett and Waters himself, through childhood, marriage, and rock stardom; all contribute to his eventual self-imposed isolation from society, each event a 'brick' in the 'wall' he builds around him.

By January 1978, Roger Waters had organised a series of songs he was writing into a conceptual form. Some months later, in July 1978, he presented the demo to each member of the band in the form of a ninety-minute cassette tape of the album (then titled *Bricks in The Wall*), along with another proposal called *The Pros and Cons of Hitchhiking*. The latter was rejected by the rest of the band and later became a Roger Waters solo album.

> We did a tour which ended I think in July or August '77 and when we finished that tour in the autumn of that year, that's when I started writing it. It took until the next July, working on my own, then I had a demo, sort of 90 minutes of stuff, which I played to the rest of the guys and then we all started working on it together, in October or November. We didn't start recording until April this year [1979], but we were rehearsing and fiddling about and obviously re-writing a lot. So it's been a long time.
>
> Roger Waters interview with Tommy Vance (1979)

> I'm not sure I can be bothered talking about *The Wall*. I think we did a damn good job on it but it slightly lacks soul for me. Our personal problems in the band by that time were becoming more dominant. Roger was becoming more dominant.
>
> David Gilmour interviewed for *The Pink Floyd and Syd Barrett Story* television documentary (2001)

The album was demoed in its entirely at least three times: once by Waters and twice by the whole band during late 1978 and early 1979 in England and France. Many of these have been released on the *Immersion* box set of *The Wall*, while others can be heard on the bootleg album *Under Construction*. Available demos and how they differ from the final released versions are discussed where relevant under each song. Producer Bob Ezrin was recruited at this time, as much to mediate between Waters and Gilmour as for his considerable skills as a musician and arranger.

The basic tracks were recorded at Super Bear Studios in the south of France, with concurrent vocal overdubs at Studio Miraval, located between Nice and Marseilles. Overdubs and mixing took place mostly at the Producers' Workshop in Los Angeles, with some work at Cherokee in Hollywood. Session musicians employed included Jeff Porcaro (drums), Lee Ritenour (guitar), Fred Mandel (Hammond organ), Bobbye Hall (percussion), Frank Marrocco (concertina), Larry Williams (clarinet), Trevor Veitch (mandolin), and Joe di Blasi (classical guitar).[3]

Released in the US a full six weeks after the UK, *The Wall* has sold around 23 million copies around the world.[4] *Rolling Stone* placed *The Wall* at number 87 on its list of 'The 500 Greatest Albums of All Time', published in 2003.

'In the Flesh?'

Roger Waters: lyrics, music, bass, VCS 3, vocals
Richard Wright: synthesisers
Nick Mason: drums
David Gilmour: guitars
Toni Tenille: backing vocals
Bruce Johnston: backing vocals

Joe Chemay: backing vocals
Stan Farber: backing vocals
Jim Haas: backing vocals
John Joyce: backing vocals
Fred Mandell: organ

One of Pink Floyd's heaviest songs, the self-parodying 'In the Flesh?' serves simultaneously as a flashback and overture to *The Wall* as the protanist, Pink, invites us to hear his story. It is reprised, with additional lyrics and no question mark, on side 4.

Originally titled 'The Show', this song was not included in Roger Waters' first demos of the songs he wrote in 1978, nor in the first full-band demos of *The Wall*; it was most likely written mid-way through pre-production. The main riff is also used in a song from *The Pros and Cons of Hitch-Hiking*, written concurrently with *The Wall*, so it is likely that Waters borrowed his own work when a new song was needed for *The Wall*. In concert, 'In the Flesh?' was performed by four backing musicians—the 'surrogate band'. [5]

'The Thin Ice'

Roger Waters: lyrics, music, bass, vocals
Richard Wright: organ, piano
Nick Mason: drums
David Gilmour: guitars, synthesisers, vocals

Written in the familiar doo-wop chord changes and sung in turn by Gilmour and Waters, 'The Thin Ice' introduces Pink as a child. Starting with a baby's cry and soft piano and ending with loud guitars, the song has immense power and a strong sense of foreboding, as well as a perhaps unconscious nod to Jethro Tull's 1974 song 'Skating Away on the Thin Ice of a New Day'.

The first and second band demos of 'The Thin Ice' are included on the *Immersion* box set.[6]

'Another Brick in the Wall, Part 1'

Roger Waters: lyrics, music, bass, vocals
Richard Wright: piano, Minimoog, Prophet-5
David Gilmour: guitars, vocals

Pink's neuroses start to build: the bricks in his wall accumulate. The three verses of 'Another Brick in the Wall' are split into three songs, each arranged in different ways.[7] This first verse is a moody reminiscence of Pink's father and his death during the Second World War; a theme that would substantially expanded on the 1983 album *The Final Cut*.

The first and second band demos of 'Another Brick in the Wall (Part 1)' are included on the *Immersion* box set.

'The Happiest Days of Our Lives'

Roger Waters: lyrics, music, bass, vocals
Richard Wright: clavinet, organ
David Gilmour: guitars, vocals
Nick Mason: drums
James Guthrie: drums

The second brick, school life, appears as Pink's emotional defences rise.

'The Happiest Days of Our Lives' appears only as part of the second set of band demos, suggesting that it was written during initial sessions for *The Wall*.

> My school life was very like that. Oh, it was awful, it was really terrible. It's not meant to be a blanket condemnation of teachers everywhere, but the bad ones can really do people in—and there were some at my school who were just incredibly bad.
>
> Roger Waters interview with Tommy Vance (1979)

'Another Brick in the Wall, Part 2'

Roger Waters: lyrics, music, bass, vocals
Richard Wright: organ, Prophet-5
Nick Mason: drums
David Gilmour: guitars, vocals
The Children of Islington Green School: vocals

Pink Floyd go disco and score a number one.

> The most important thing I did for the song was to insist that it be more than just one verse and one chorus long. When we played it with the disco drumbeat I said: 'Man, this is a hit! But it's one minute 20. We need two verses and two choruses.' We were able to copy the first verse and chorus, take one of the drum fills and put it in between. Then the question is what do you do with the second verse, which is the same? I've got this thing about kids on record. So while we were in America, we sent [recording engineer] Nick Griffiths to a school near the Floyd studios [in Islington, North London]. I said, 'Give me 24 tracks of kids singing this thing. I want Cockney, I want posh, fill 'em up' and I put them on the song. I called Roger into the room and when the kids came in on the second verse there was a total softening of his face and you just knew that he knew it was going to be an important record.
>
> Bob Ezrin, *Guitar World* (2009)

> I think their attitude toward singles had changed over the years. Particularly since 'Money' had received so much air play without initially being released as a single. As the album took shape, 'Brick 2' was clearly the best choice for a first single. We were not trying to make it blatantly commercial, just a good groove.
>
> James Guthrie, *Hey You* (2005)

Gilmour's fluid and melodic guitar solo was played in a single take on a Gibson Les Paul, a model not otherwise associated with the pro-Fender guitarist.

Released as a single on 16 November 1979, there are four extra bars at the beginning, a rhythm guitar introduction that does not appear on the album because of the abrupt transition from 'The Happiest Days of Our Lives'. It fades sooner than the album version, too. A different edit is available on the *A Collection of Great Dance Songs* compilation, released 23 November 1981: this has the same four bars intro as the single version, but includes the whole of the guitar solo.

Part of the concept from the beginning—the brick in question being eduction—three different demos are included in the *Immersion* box set.

'Mother'

Roger Waters: lyrics, music, acoustic guitar, vocals
David Gilmour: guitars, bass, vocals
Bob Ezrin: organ, piano and synthesiser
Jeff Porcaro: drums

Neurosis number three. 'Mother' combines folky verses—starting quietly with voice and a single acoustic guitar, with a gradual expansion of its instrumentation to include organ, piano, drums, bass—and a loud, expressive guitar solo. Lead vocals are from Waters and Gilmour, each taking separate section as with other songs on *The Wall* such as 'The Thin Ice', 'Comfortably Numb' and 'Hey You'.

'Mother' is notable for its varied use of time signatures, such as 5/8 and 9/8. Nick Mason relinquished the drumming duties to session drummer Jeff Porcaro.[8]

> Nick worked hard and played well on *The Wall*. But there was one track called 'Mother' which he really didn't get. So I hired Jeff Porcaro to do it. And Roger latched on to this idea and began to think, is Nick really necessary?
>
> David Gilmour, *Mojo* (May 1994)

Part of the concept from the beginning, three different demos are included in the *Immersion* box set.[9] A partially rerecorded version of this song with different verses

Pink Floyd's debut album, *The Piper at the Gates of Dawn*, released in August 1967. A 1997 copy of *Record Mirror* commented: 'The psychedelic image of the group really comes to life on this LP, which is a fine showcase for both their talent and the recording technique. Plenty of mind-blowing sound.' (*Warner Music Group/ Parlophone*)

The 'Apples and Oranges' and 'Paint Box' single was Pink Floyd's follow-up to 'See Emily Play'. 'Apples and Oranges' is early-Floyd-by-numbers, but 'Paint Box' shows Richard Wright's emerging songwriting talents and was the band's first comment on the vagaries of fame—later explored at length in songs from *Atom Heart Mother*, *Wish You Were Here*, and, notably, *The Wall*. (*Warner Music Group/Parlophone*)

A schizophrenic album, *A Saucerful of Secrets* was recorded over a period of several months. Sessions in August, October, November, and December 1967, and sporadic recording in January, February and April 1968 resulted in a mixed bag of tracks, with Syd Barrett only present on 'Set the Controls for the Heart of the Sun' and his own, valedictory 'Jugband Blues'. (*Warner Music Group/Parlophone*)

Jim Miller, *Rolling Stone* (October 1968): 'With [Syd] Barrett gone we are left with the work of bassist Roger Waters and organist Rick Wright. Waters (who wrote a couple of dull tracks on the first album) is an uninteresting writer, vocalist and bass player. The production work is not as glittery as the first album's and the instrumental work is shoddy and routine.' (*Warner Music Group/Parlophone*)

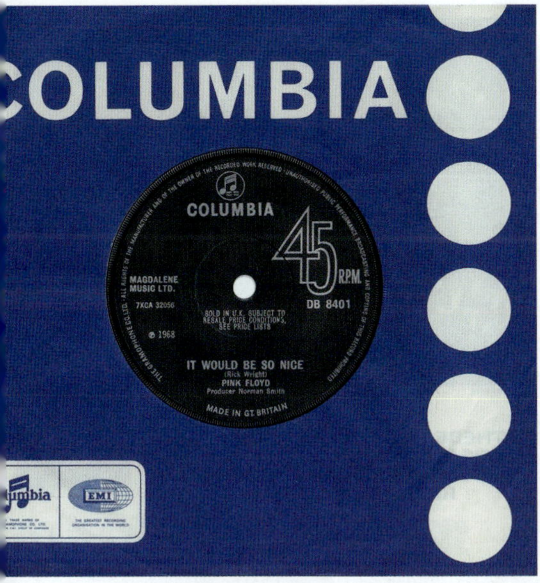

Above: 'It Would Be So Nice' (April 1968) and 'Point Me at the Sky' (December 1968)—the last two songs recorded by Pink Floyd for single-only releases for fourteen years.(*Warner Music Group/Parlophone*)

Below: *AllMusic*: 'Commissioned as a soundtrack to the seldom-seen French hippie movie of the same name, *More* was a Pink Floyd album in its own right, reaching the Top Ten in Britain. The group's atmospheric music was a natural for movies, but when assembled for record, these pieces were unavoidably a bit patchwork, ranging from folky ballads to fierce electronic instrumentals to incidental mood music.' (*Warner Music Group/Parlophone*)

Alan Styles and Peter Watts
with the band's equipment at
Biggin Hill Airport, 1969.
(*Warner Music Group/Parlophone*)

Above: Rolling Stone (September 2013): '[*Ummagumma*] begins with a live rendition of Syd Barrett's 'Astronomy Domine' and then moves forward through their brief career with works like 'Set the Controls for the Heart of the Sun' and 'A Saucerful of Secrets'. Casual fans who love 'Wish You Were Here' and 'Money' may not find much to love here, but to the truly devoted *Ummagumma* is Pink Floyd at the peak of their ambitious weirdness.' (*Warner Music Group/Parlophone*)

A bizarre collection of antiques and curios, *Relics* was the first of seemingly endless repackaging of Pink Floyd's back catalogue. It remains the only source of the complete EMI studio version of 'Interstellar Overdrive'. (*Warner Music Group/Parlophone*)

Picnic – A Breath of Fresh Air, a sampler issued by the Harvest Records label in 1970. The previously unreleased (and unfinished) Pink Floyd song 'Embryo' was included on the album without the band's permission. (*Warner Music Group/ Parlophone*)

Previous below: Alec Dubro, *Rolling Stone* (December 1970): '*Atom Heart Mother* is a step headlong into the last century and a dissipation of [Pink Floyd's] collective talents, which are considerable. Side one is a suite, almost a symphony. It has a lot in it. They use orchestral elements and a choir. The best that can be said for it is that it's craftsman-like and that in spite of its many parts, it's an entity. But that's all.' (*Warner Music Group/Parlophone*)

Daryl Easlea, *BBC Music* (2007): '*Meddle* represents the birth of Pink Floyd as we know them today. This is everything right about progressive rock; engaging, intelligent and compelling.' (*Warner Music Group/ Parlophone*)

Ric Albano, *Classic Rock Review* (2012): 'One of the lost treasures of classic rock and, by far, the most overlooked album in the Pink Floyd catalogue during their classic era, *Obscured by Clouds* acted as a mere warm-up for the more ambitious and highly-regarded *The Dark Side of the Moon*.' (*Warner Music Group/ Parlophone*)

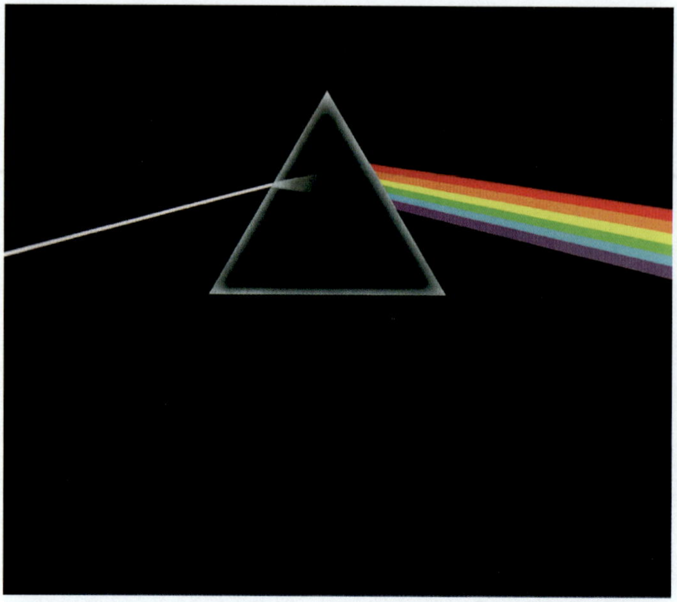

Nicholas Lezard, *The Guardian* (9 April 2013): 'If it is not exactly the most feel-good party record you've ever heard, [*The Dark Side of the Moon*] works perfectly on its own terms, ends superbly, and, with 10 tracks on it, is positively sprightly when you compare it with some of their other work, whose length, you feel, was constrained only by the limited amount of vinyl on one side of an album.' (*Warner Music Group/ Parlophone*)

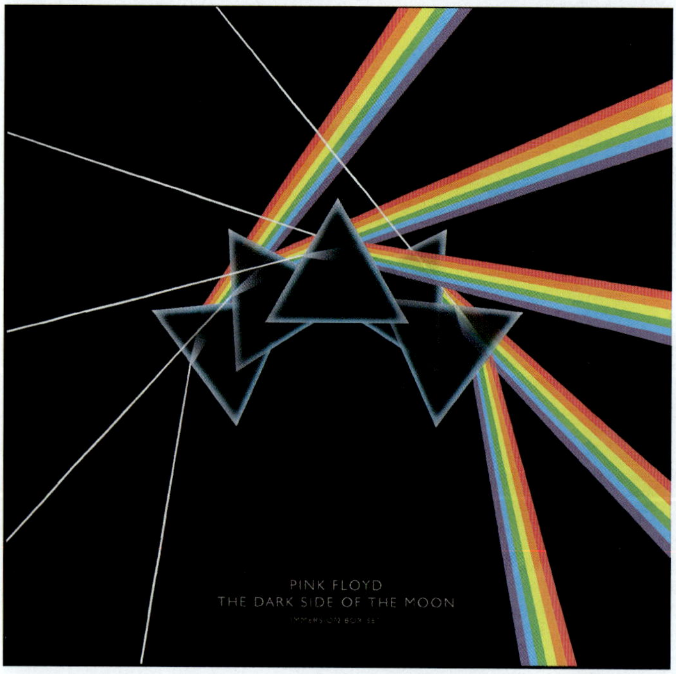

The expanded collector's edition of *The Dark Side of the Moon* with memorabilia and previously unreleased material. Positives: the entire album recorded live at the Empire Pool, Wembley in November 1974. Negatives: a scarf and some marbles. (*Warner Music Group/ Parlophone*)

Opposite top: Robert Christgau, *Village Voice* (1975): 'No dumb tribulations-of-a-rock-star epic here—the dedication to long-departed crazy Syd Barrett gives it an emotional resolve that mitigates what little self-pity lyricist Roger Waters allows himself. Even more remarkable, the music is not only simple and attractive, with the synthesizer used mostly for texture and the guitar breaks for comment, but it actually achieves some of the symphonic dignity (and cross-referencing) that *The Dark Side of the Moon* simulated so ponderously.' (*Warner Music Group/Parlophone*)

The expanded collector's editions of *Wish You Were* with memorabilia and previously unreleased material. Positives: 5.1 surround sound mix and Stéphane Grappelli on violin. Negatives: another scarf and some more marbles. (*Warner Music Group/Parlophone*)

The artwork of Hipgnosis defines mid-period Pink Floyd. This empty suit, shot in the Yuma Desert in California, emphasises the album's theme of absence. (*Warner Music Group/Parlophone*)

The pig flies again over Battersea Power Station to promote the 2011 series of Pink Floyd re-releases. *(Warner Music Group/Parlophone)*

Below left: Kurt Loder, *Rolling Stone* (February 1980): 'While *The Wall*'s length is certainly justified by the breadth of its thematic concerns, the music is stretched a bit thin. Heavy-metal maestro Bob Ezrin adds a certain hard-rock consciousness to a few cuts but has generally been unable to match the high sonic gloss that Alan Parsons contributed to *The Dark Side of the Moon*. Even Floyd starved devotees may not be sucked into *The Wall*'s relatively flat aural ambiance on first hearing. But when they finally are they may wonder which way is out real fast.' (*Warner Music Group/Parlophone*)

Below right: The hit! 'Another Brick in the Wall Part 2' picture sleeve. (*Warner Music Group/Parlophone*)

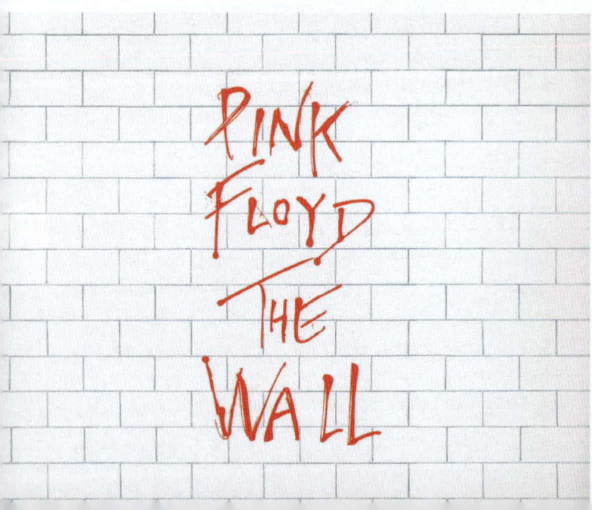

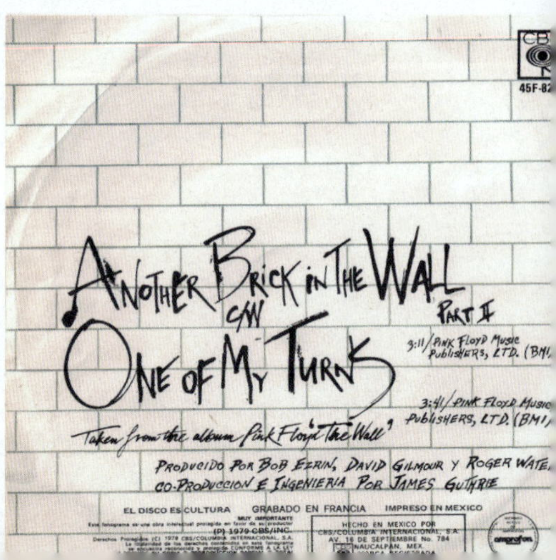

While hardly the most uplifting listen, there is much to enjoy and even more to admire in the last Pink Floyd album to feature Roger Waters. It's Waters' *de facto* debut solo album, and, lyrically, may well be his finest hour. In the final analysis, if the previous four Pink Floyd albums, from *The Dark Side of the Moon* through to *The Wall*, are their collective definitive statements, then *The Final Cut* is Waters'. (*Warner Music Group/Parlophone*)

Rachel Mann, *The Quietus* (June 2013): 'If Floyd had famously been falling apart for years, under stress from the conflicting egos of Waters and Gilmour, it's not unreasonable to suggest that *The Final Cut* is, from the title down, the ultimate public statement of a band's collapse into self-indulgence and failure. It is certainly a candidate for most depressing album of the 80s.' (*Warner Music Group/Parlophone*)

Previous above: Billboard (1977): 'Pink Floyd's rare gift is to be at its most commercial when it is being most true to its obscure, menacing, surrealistic vision. Its latest is a symbolic concept album that divides humanity into manipulative, lonely dogs, comically depressing pig rulers and rebellious sheep. Loving communion is the only way to rise above this animalistic existence, as expressed in a brief, quiet acoustic interlude that opens and closes the LP. The rest of the album consists of three ominously driving long songs which alternate intense instrumental passages with those quirky, sardonic lyrics.' *(Warner Music Group/Parlophone)*

Cory Garcia, *Houston Press* (2012): '[*A Momentary Lapse of Reason*] makes for a frustrating listen because buried behind the long intros and unnecessary sound effects is the foundation of what could be a good record.'
(*Warner Music Group/Parlophone*)

Tom Graves, *Rolling Stone* (16 June 1994): '*The Division Bell* is a quieter, more atmospheric and contemplative Pink Floyd, with lyrics so opaque and inert one cannot hope to plumb their meaning. The album gives off the uncomfortable whiff of middle-age and greying sensibilities. Gilmour, who has become Pink Floyd's de facto leader, in particular seems bored or dispirited. His guitar solos were once the band's centrepieces, as articulate, melodic and well-defined as any in rock. No longer. He now has settled into rambling, indistinct asides that are as forgettable as they used to be indelible.'
(*Warner Music Group/Parlophone*)

Andy Gill, *The Independent* (5 November 2014): 'Depressingly symptomatic of the stasis that a certain kind of ponderous prog-rock had reached by the late '70s. It's just aimless jamming, one long thread of Dave Gilmour's guitar against Rick Wright's pastel keyboards and Nick Mason's tentative percussion, with nary a melody of any distinction alighted upon for the duration. It would take a Barrett-load of drugs to make this sound remotely interesting, though I wouldn't advise that. But what's blindingly clear is that, without the sparking creativity of a Syd or Roger, all that's left is ghastly faux-psychedelic dinner-party muzak. Which is fine, if you're thinking of throwing a ghastly faux-psychedelic dinner-party.' (*Warner Music Group/Parlophone*)

David Fricke, *Rolling Stone* (7 November 2014): 'A suite of mostly instrumental moods and fragments, *The Endless River* rolls like a requiem through familiar echoes. The effect is inevitably cinematic, a fluid rewind to the Floyd's early film scores. 'Louder Than Words', the closing vocal track, is undercut by slang in the first lines. But when Gilmour sings, 'The beat of our hearts/ Is louder than words,' it feels, again, like hanging on—with grace. This album is an unexpected, welcome epitaph.' (*Warner Music Group/Parlophone*)

Above: Roger Waters toured a full production of *The Wall* across the world in 2010–2013, with 219 performances in total—making it the highest grossing tour for a solo artist of all time. (*Neil Palfreyman*)

Below: David Gilmour continues to tour and make occasional guest appearances, including a 2012 'virtual birthday party' for his old friend the late Douglas Adams. (*Paul Hudson*)

was used on the soundtrack of the film *Pink Floyd—The Wall*, released in July 1982. The lyric 'Is it just a waste of time?' from the original album is replaced with 'Mother, am I really dying?' which is how this line appeared on the original LP lyric sheet.

'Goodbye Blue Sky'

Roger Waters: lyrics, music, VCS 3
Richard Wright: synthesiser
David Gilmour: guitars, bass, synthesiser, vocals
Harry Waters: child's voice

What sounds like a Gilmour arrangement, all nylon-strung guitars and vocal harmonies, is pure Waters, as evidenced in the original home demo where all chords and lyrics are in place.

A rewrite of themes heard in 'Childhood's End', looking back on childhood and looking forward to the rest of your life, 'Goodbye Blue Sky' is one of those songs that hides a stark message behind a bright tune and uplifting arrangement.

Part of the concept from the beginning, two demos are included in the Immersion box set. A third can be heard on the bootleg album *Under Construction*.

'Empty Spaces'

Roger Waters: lyrics, music, bass, VCS 3, vocals
Richard Wright: piano
David Gilmour: guitars, clavinet, string synthesiser, Prophet-5
James Guthrie: string synthesiser

A long, eerie instrumental with a semi-spoken verse, it has the same backing track as the first half of 'What Shall We Do Now?' which was planned for side two but dropped—the lyrics are printed on the album's inner sleeve.

Part of the concept from the beginning, two different demos are included in the *Immersion* box set.

Not performed live: replaced by 'What Shall We Do Now?' in live concerts and on the soundtrack to *Pink Floyd—The Wall*.

'Young Lust'

Roger Waters: music, lyrics, vocals
Richard Wright: organ, electric piano
Nick Mason: drums
David Gilmour: music, guitars, bass, vocals

Pink throws himself headlong into the hedonism of sex, drugs, and rock and roll.

'Young Lust' is a heavy rocker, sung and played with aggression by David Gilmour. The music and lyrics for the chorus were written by Roger Waters and part of his original demo of this is available on the *Immersion* box set of *The Wall*. The music for the verses was written by Gilmour and a second version with these verses but different lyrics is also in this box set. A complete instrumental run-through, very close to the released arrangement, is on the bootleg album *Under Construction*.

> 'Young Lust' reminds me very much of a song we recorded years and years ago called 'The Nile Song'. It's very similar, Dave sings it in a very similar way. I love the vocals. But it's meant to be a pastiche of any young rock and roll band out on the road.
>
> Roger Waters interview with Tommy Vance (1979)

The single edit uses a 4-bar drum intro not heard elsewhere and continues to a hard stop at the end, without the partial fade or telephone call sound effects.

'One of My Turns'

Roger Waters: lyrics, music, bass, vocals
Richard Wright: piano
Nick Mason: drums, percussion
David Gilmour: guitar
Lee Ritentour: guitar
Bob Ezrin: organ, Prophet-5
Trudy Young: voice of the groupie

Pink takes a groupie back to his hotel room ('are all these your guitars?') after hearing of his wife's affair at the end of 'Young Lust'. He explodes in a fit of violence, destroying the room. Sung in Waters' highest register, Pink's anguish and self-pity are wrought in every syllable.

'One of My Turns' is one of a handful of songs on *The Wall* where guitar overdubs were performed by Los Angeles session musician Lee Ritentour. The song is in the second set of band demos included in the *Immersion* box set, so it was most likely written after recording sessions began.

'One of My Turns' was released as the B-side to 'Another Brick in the Wall, Part 2' on 23 November 1979 and therefore, along with its A-side, it was one of the first songs from the project to be heard publicly.

'Don't Leave Me Now'

Roger Waters: lyrics, music, guitar, VCS 3, vocals
Richard Wright: bass pedals, organ, piano, and synthesiser
Nick Mason: drums, percussion
David Gilmour: bass, guitars, vocals

A slow, dissonant, disjointed song reflecting Pink's dysfunction and depression as he pleads to his wife to stay with him. Happy days.

Part of the concept from the beginning, three different demos are included in the *Immersion* box set.

> A very depressing song. I love it!
>
> Roger Waters interview with Tommy Vance (1979)

'Another Brick in the Wall, Part 3'

Roger Waters: lyrics, music, bass, guitar, synthesiser, vocals
Richard Wright: Prophet-5
Nick Mason: drums
David Gilmour: guitars, synthesiser

A thumping up-tempo third verse: Pink's isolation builds. Intended to be part of the concept from the beginning (working title 'Drugs'), three different demos are included in the Immersion box set.

'Goodbye Cruel World'

Roger Waters: lyrics, music, bass, vocals
Richard Wright: Prophet-5

> That's him going catatonic. He's just curling up and he's not going to move. That's it, he's had enough, that's the end.
>
> Roger Waters interview with Tommy Vance (1979)

Part of the concept from the beginning, three different demos are included in the *Immersion* box set.

'Hey You'

Roger Waters: lyrics, music, vocals
Richard Wright: organ, piano, and synthesiser
Nick Mason: drums
David Gilmour: guitars, bass, pedal steel, vocals

One of the key songs in Pink Floyd's catalogue, seemingly a plea for connection and contact between individuals, 'Hey You' is beautifully written, arranged, and produced. It is a rare example of a genuinely human song with some of Waters' best lyrics, utilising an impeccable metaphor of negativity as a 'stone', or a weight that we must carry, carried over from 'Dogs' on *Animals*.

The crystalline opening section of 'Hey You' is a cunning rewrite of 'A Pillow of Winds' from *Meddle*, employing the same guitar arpeggios and bubbling fretless bass. The familiar use of dynamics powers the central section as Gilmour's guitar soars over a heavy reprise of the melody from 'Another Brick in the Wall'. Gilmour's warm, low vocals in the first half of the song contrast markedly with Waters' higher, brittle singing after the guitar solo.

Part of the concept from the beginning, two demos are included in the *Immersion* box set: Waters' home demo, and a much later pre-production version that is not so different to the released take.

> Bob Ezrin called me and he said, 'I've just listened to side three and it doesn't work'. I'd been feeling uncomfortable about it anyway. I realised that 'Hey You' could conceptually go anywhere and it would make a much better side if we put it at the front. That decision was made very late.
>
> Roger Waters interview with Tommy Vance (1979)

'Is There Anybody Out There?'

Roger Waters: lyrics, music, bass, vocals
Richard Wright: Prophet-5
David Gilmour: vocals
Joe DiBlasi: classical guitar
Bob Ezrin: synthesisers

A song of two halves. A droning synthesiser, the squealing guitar effects from 'Echoes', and a chanted question preludes a second half comprising an orchestrated classical guitar solo. The gorgeous, melancholic classical guitar line was played by Joe DiBlasi during the orchestral sessions in New York.

Part of the concept from the beginning, two demos are included in the *Immersion* box set, the second with the familiar classical guitar pattern. A third demo, much shorter and presumably pre-dating this can be heard on the bootleg album *Under Construction*.

A partially rerecorded version of this song, with Gilmour performing the classical guitar part, was used on the soundtrack of the film *Pink Floyd—The Wall*, released in July 1982.

'Nobody Home'

Roger Waters: lyrics, music, VSC 3, vocals
Richard Wright: Prophet-5
David Gilmour: bass
Bob Ezrin: piano
The New York Philharmonic Orchestra

Pink is withdrawn, with the world beyond his reach.

Written during recording sessions, most likely the last song to be written for *The Wall*, much of 'Nobody Home' describes Syd Barrett's fragile mental state during 1967—the lyrics are almost a third person rewrite of Barrett's 'Vegetable Man'—as well as references to Richard Wright ('Got a grand piano to prop up my mortal remains') and Waters himself. One of the best songs from *The Wall*, 'Nobody Home' is almost heartbreakingly delivered, comprising Waters' cracked vocal, Bob Ezrin's lyrical piano, and full orchestral accompaniment.

> Some of the songs—I remember 'Nobody Home'—came along when we well into the thing and [Roger had] gone off in a sulk the night before and come in the next day with something fantastic. It's often good to be geed up into a little state of rage.
>
> David Gilmour, *Mojo* (December 1999)

'Vera'

Roger Waters: lyrics, music, vocals
Richard Wright: Prophet-5
Nick Mason: drums
David Gilmour: guitars, bass
The New York Philharmonic Orchestra

A short tribute to the British wartime singer Vera Lynn. The opening dialogue ('Where the hell are you, Simon?') and the sound effects are from the 1969 film *The Battle of Britain*.

Part of the concept from the beginning, two demos are included in the *Immersion* box set.

'Bring the Boys Back Home'

Roger Waters: lyrics, music, vocals
Jeff Porcaro: snare drum
Military drum corps
The New York Philharmonic Orchestra
The choir of the New York Opera

> It's partly about not letting people go off and be killed in wars, but it's partly about not allowing rock and roll, or making cars, or selling soap, or getting involved in biological research, or anything that anybody might do … not letting that become such an important and 'jolly boy's game' that it becomes more important than friends, wives, children, or other people.
>
> Roger Waters interview with Tommy Vance (1979)

Part of the concept from the beginning, two demos are included in the *Immersion* box set. A rerecorded version of this song taken from the soundtrack of the film was released as the B-side to 'When the Tigers Broke Free' on 26 July 1982 and on the soundtrack of the film *Pink Floyd—The Wall*, released in July 1982.

'Comfortably Numb'

Roger Waters: lyrics, bass, vocals
Richard Wright: organ
Nick Mason: drums
David Gilmour: music, guitars, bass, pedal steel, vocals
Lee Ritentour: acoustic guitar
The New York Philharmonic Orchestra

Pink is filled with drugs to enable him to perform a concert.

'Comfortably Numb' is perhaps the most famous Pink Floyd song of all. It is a true collaboration between Roger Waters and David Gilmour.

> In its finished state, 'Comfortably Numb' is Pink Floyd's A Day in the Life—the song on which the band's two chief creative forces came together at their absolute best.
>
> Dan Wiencek, *Popdose.com* (February 2012)

Waters wrote the lyrics, with many revisions as the album progressed, and Gilmour wrote the music.

> In the songbook against 'Comfortably Numb' it says 'music by Gilmour and Waters'. It shouldn't. He did the lyrics. I did the music. I kept finding hundreds of little things like that. Shouldn't bitch, but one does feel unjustly done.
>
> David Gilmour, *Mojo* (May 1994)

Called 'The Doctor' until the album was almost complete, part of the lyric comes from Waters' own experience recording *The Dark Side of the Moon* in 1972.

> I can remember being in the canteen at Abbey Road and suddenly there was no pain; everything—the table, all the people at it—receded. The sound became tinny and the room looked like I was looking at something through the wrong end of a pair of binoculars. I thought to myself, 'Wow, this is what it's like to go mad.'
>
> Roger Waters quoted in *The Dark Side of the Moon: The Making of Pink Floyd's Masterpiece* (2005)

There are four known demo versions, each unique in some way.

David Gilmour's Home Demo (3:14)

Just the music for the chorus and verse with Gilmour humming the melody. Available for years as an off-the-air snippet (it had been broadcast during an interview for BBC Radio One, on July 28, 1992) it was released, with a cleaner sound and seemingly complete, on the *Immersion* box set in 2012.

'First Band Demo' (3:15)

The structure of this demo is the same as the first half of the finished version. After the familiar intro, the first verse has a double-tracked Waters, both singing the lyrics (right stereo channel) and portraying a ranting doctor (left stereo channel). The chorus, sung by Gilmour, has the same magnificent lyrics as the finished version and the first guitar solo is almost note-for-note the same as the familiar release.[10] The second verse, sung by Waters, again with different lyrics, has a natural ending. There is no second chorus and no second guitar solo. It was released on the *Immersion* box set in 2012.

> Verse one: Come in, sit down / Can you show me where it hurts? / Try to tell me / Using your own words. / I must seem very old / But I was young once too / I've seen a lot of boys like you / I always say the same thing
>
> Verse two: You've got to pull yourself together / You shouldn't let it get you down / You ought to take it like a man / You should go out and do the town / It's no good

moping here alone / Feeling sorry for yourself / Go out and see what you can find / It's Saturday night you must unwind

'Second Band Demo' (3:15)

This second band demo uses essentially the same backing track as the first—there are a few extra keyboard sounds—but with different lyrics in the verses. Gilmour sings throughout but with no enthusiasm or commitment whatsoever. The first verse has mostly new lyrics with the line 'Can/if you show me where it hurts?' retained through all three sets of demo lyrics. The second verse is mostly the same as the first band demo.

> Verse one: What seems to be the trouble? / Are we feeling out of sorts? / Did you think they'd gone forever? / Can you show me where it hurts? / I think I know what's wrong / A lot of people get this way / Take two of these four times daily / I'll drop in when I pass this way again

> Verse two: You have to pull yourself together / You have to take it like a man / You mustn't let it get your head down / You should go out and do the town / It's no good moping here alone / Feeling sorry for yourself / Go and see what you can find / It Saturday night you should unwind

'Final Band Demo' (4:14)

A fourth version, much closer to the finished version, can be heard on the bootleg album *Under Construction*. It uses almost the same musical structure as the official release on *The Wall* (intro / first verse / chorus / guitar solo over chorus chords / second verse (but no second chorus) / guitar solo over verse chords) and the same lyrics in the choruses. Waters has rewritten the verses once again and they are now much closer to the familiar lyrics on the released album.

> Verse one: Hello, is there anybody in there? / Is anybody bleeding? / Is there anyone at home? / Come on, I know you're hiding / I could hear you're screaming / Your neighbours called me on the phone. / Listen. I am a physician and I can handle your condition like a magician / If you show me where it hurts

> Verse two: Wake up now, pull yourself together / Get out and meet new people / I'm sure they'll understand / Come on, put away the shotgun / Yeah, have another blue one / Have your fingertips gone numb? / Goodbye, try and see the bright side / Listen to some pop groups, rock and roll / Go out and see some shows

As this song was not part of Roger Waters' original concept, there is no recording from his home demo sessions in 1978.

The final version has Gilmour's warm vocals, with acoustic guitar and orchestra in the chorus, and Waters singing the verses within his range against strong electric guitar backing. It is well documented that Waters and Gilmour disagreed with the production arrangement on this song—Waters wanted a lush, orchestral backing; Gilmour wanted a harder, guitar-based track. In the end, a mix of the two versions was used: the cross-fade is obvious from 4:55 to 4:59 of the studio cut.[11]

Then, of course, there is that guitar solo.

> One of the most emotive and transcendentally powerful pieces of guitar soloing ever recorded.
>
> Cliff Jones, *Echoes* (1996)

In August 2006, it was voted the greatest guitar solo of all time in a poll by listeners of digital radio station Planet Rock. Who am I to argue?

> I banged out five or six solos and followed my usual procedure, which is to listen back to each solo and make a chart, noting which bits are good. Then I create one great composite solo by whipping one fader up, then another fader, jumping from phrase to phrase until everything flows together.
>
> David Gilmour, quoted in *Guitar World* (March 2016)

'Comfortably Numb' was the last song ever to be performed by Waters, Gilmour, Wright, and Mason together, at Live 8 on 2 July 2005. The song has also been performed on most of Waters' and Gilmour's solo tours since 1985.[12]

'The Show Must Go On'

Roger Waters: lyrics, music
Richard Wright: synthesisers
Nick Mason: drums
David Gilmour: guitars, bass, vocals
Bob Ezrin: piano, synthesiser
Toni Tenille: backing vocals
Bruce Johnston: backing vocals
Joe Chemay: backing vocals
Stan Farber: backing vocals
Jim Haas: backing vocals
John Joyce: backing vocals

Pink prepares himself for a performance—the reprise of 'In the Flesh'.

It is the only song from the finished album on which Waters does not perform.

Two versions of 'The Show Must Go On' were included in the series of demos on the *Immersion* box set. The final demo also has an extra verse that was cut from the studio album—this appears in the lyrics on the inner sleeve and was performed in live concerts in 1980–81.

> Do I have to stand up / Wild eyed in the spotlight
> What a nightmare / Why don't I turn and run?

A further demo (available on the bootleg *Under Construction*) has another unused lyrical section, sung by Waters.

> It's OK now, you're a blackbelt / The worms have fled the rising sun
> The evil power is on the way / Forget the past, start again

There were plans for the Beach Boys to record backing vocals for this song (and two others), but, in the event, only Bruce Johnston was able to attend.

'In the Flesh'

Roger Waters: lyrics, music, bass, VCS 3, vocals
Nick Mason: drums
David Gilmour: guitars, synthesiser
Bob Ezrin: synthesiser
Fred Mandell: organ
Toni Tenille: backing vocals
Bruce Johnston: backing vocals
Joe Chemay: backing vocals
Stan Farber: backing vocals
Jim Haas: backing vocals
John Joyce: backing vocals

Pink is in a drug-induced hallucination and believes himself to be a fascist dictator as his concert is transformed to a political rally. 'In the Flesh' is a reprise of the opening song from the album but with a longer, quieter lyrical section and decidedly antagonistic lyrics.

'Run Like Hell'

Roger Waters: lyrics, vocals
Richard Wright: Prophet-5
Nick Mason: drums

David Gilmour: music, guitars, bass, vocals
Bobbye Hall: percussion

The music for 'Run Like Hell' was written by David Gilmour—his instrumental demo can be heard on the *Immersion* Box Set—and was added to a snarling Waters lyric and disco beat. The song is characterised by a delayed guitar setting, allowing overlapping rhythmic echoes of sound; this same effect can also be heard on 'The Hero's Return', 'One Slip', 'Take It Back' and 'Allons-Y'.[13]

Released as a single in some territories on 17 April 1980.

'Waiting for the Worms'

Roger Waters: lyrics, music, VCS 3, vocals
Nick Mason: drums
Richard Wright: organ
David Gilmour: guitars, bass, synthesiser, vocals
Bob Ezrin: piano, vocals
Toni Tenille: backing vocals
Bruce Johnston: backing vocals
Joe Chemay: backing vocals
Stan Farber: backing vocals
Jim Haas: backing vocals
John Joyce: backing vocals

Pink is steadily going insane as his dictator persona starts to take over.

Starting as a slow march, it later utilises the same churning musical theme heard in 'Another Brick in the Wall', 'Hey You', and 'The Trial'.

> The worms have a lot less to do with the piece than they did a year ago; a year ago they were very much a part of it, if you like they were my symbolic representation of decay. Because the basic idea the whole thing really is that if you isolate yourself you decay.
>
> Roger Waters interview with Tommy Vance (1979)

'Stop'

Roger Waters: lyrics, music, vocals
Bob Ezrin: piano

Pink snaps out of his delusion and determines to find out why he has fallen so far. 'Stop' is a short linking piece, with tinkly piano and very direct lyrics.

> At the end of 'Waiting for the Worms' it gets too much for him, the oppression and he says 'stop.' It's very quick and then he says 'I wanna go home, take off this uniform and leave the show,' but he says 'I'm waiting in this prison cell because I have to know, have I been guilty all this time' and then he tries himself if you like.
>
> Roger Waters interview with Tommy Vance (1979)

In the version used in the film *Pink Floyd—The Wall,* we get to hear snippets from two then-unreleased Waters' lyrics: 'Your Possible Pasts' (written as part of *The Wall* but not used until *The Final Cut*), and '5:11am (The Moment of Clarity)'.

'The Trial'

Roger Waters: lyrics, music, vocals
Nick Mason: bass drum, cymbals
David Gilmour: guitars, bass
Bob Ezrin: music: piano
'Vicky' and 'Clare': vocals
The New York Philharmonic Orchestra

The climax of the album. As Pink's mental state hangs in the balance he is confronted by his life's primary influences—mother, teacher, wife—then the judge who declares sentence. Waters sings the dialogue for each character in different accents against a grandiose orchestral backing. The song ends with the sound of a wall being demolished amid chants of 'Tear down the wall!' marking the destruction of Pink's metaphorical wall as he exorcises his demons.

There is a lyrical echo of *Atom Heart Mother*'s 'If'—'if I were a good man I would talk to you more often that I do' becomes 'you should have talked to me more often than you did, but no!'

'Outside the Wall'

Roger Waters: lyrics, music, vocals
David Gilmour: vocals
Trevor Veitch: mandolin
Larry Williams: clarinet
An uncredited children's choir

The album's resolution marries a slow concertina and clarinet with an opaque Waters lyric which does not so much close out the narrative as leave it open to interpretation. The final words heard are 'isn't this where…', which link back to the opening words from 'In the Flesh?': '…we came in', thus bringing the story and the album full circle.

Unreleased / Unused Songs

'Prelude (Vera Lynn)'

Written by Roger Waters.

A short snatch of Vera Lynn singing 'We'll Meet Again' that would not be used on the final album, despite being included on Waters' home demo as well as the band's early demo recordings. This concept was revisited in the film *Pink Floyd—The Wall*, which opens with Lynn singing 'The Little Boy That Santa Claus Forgot'.

'Teacher, Teacher'

Written by Roger Waters.

Replaced by 'The Happiest Days of Our Lives' on the final album, 'Teacher Teacher' is musically similar to the later 'The Hero's Return'.

'(It's) Never Too Late'

Written by Roger Waters.

A short reprise/prelude of the musical theme from 'Outside the Wall', included as part of the band demos on the *Immersion* box set. The melody and some of the words were later included within the film soundtrack version of 'Outside the Wall' and on 'Southampton Dock' from *The Final Cut*.

'What Shall We Do Now?'

Written by Roger Waters.

> Now that's the track that's not on the album. It's quite long and this side was too long and there was too much of it.
>
> Roger Waters interview with Tommy Vance (1979)

The full-length version of 'Empty Spaces' leads to an urgent, powerful rocker which was dropped so late that the album's inner sleeve not only features the song in its track listing, but also includes its lyrics.

> Shall we buy a new guitar? / Shall we drive a more powerful car? / Shall we work straight through the night? / Shall we get into fights? / Leave the lights on? / Drop bombs? / Do tours of the east? / Contract diseases? / Bury bones? / Break up homes?

/ Send flowers by phone? / Take to drink? / Go to shrinks? / Give up meat? / Rarely sleep? / Keep people as pets? / Train dogs? / Race rats? / Fill the attic with cash? / Bury treasure? / Store up leisure? / But never relax at all / With our backs to the wall.

This song was used on the soundtrack of the film *Pink Floyd—The Wall*, released in July 1982, and in concert in 1980 and 1981.

'Sexual Revolution'

Written by Roger Waters.

Included in the first full-band demo of *The Wall*, but dropped and re-used on Waters' solo album *The Pros and Cons of Hitch Hiking*.

'The Last Few Bricks'

Written by Roger Waters and David Gilmour.

An instrumental bridge/medley used by Pink Floyd and Roger Waters at *The Wall* live shows in 1980–81 and 2010–13. It was composed to allow the band's roadies time to finish constructing the wall after 'Another Brick in the Wall, Part 3' and before Waters appeared in the last brick-wide space in the wall to sing 'Goodbye Cruel World'.

'The Last Few Bricks' contains themes from 'The Happiest Days of Our Lives', 'Don't Leave Me Now', 'Young Lust', 'Empty Spaces', and, on occasion, a jam similar to 'Any Colour You Like'.

Live Performances

The entire album, including 'What Shall We Do Now?' and 'The Last Few Bricks' was performed at all of Pink Floyd's complete run-throughs of *The Wall* in 1980 and 1981. A reconstructed version of the show can be heard on *Is There Anybody Out There? The Wall Live 1980–81* (released 23 March 2001) and also on the *Immersion* box set of *The Wall* (27 February 2012). With the following exceptions, all of the songs on this album were recorded on 7 August 1980:

'The Last Few Bricks', edited from shows on 7 August 1980 and 9 August 1980;
'The Thin Ice', edited from shows on 7 August 1980 and 13 June 1981;
'Another Brick in the Wall, Part 2', edited from shows on 8 August 1980, 9 August 1980, and 14 June 1981;
'Outside the Wall', edited from performances on 8 and 9 August 1980;
'Nobody Home', edited from performances on 8 August 1980 and 15 June 1981;
'Goodbye Cruel World', 'Stop' and 'The Trial', 9 August 1980;

'Comfortably Numb', edited from performances on 9 August 1980 and 15 June 1981;
'Vera' and 'Waiting for the Worms', 13 June 1981;
'What Shall We Do Now?', 14 June 1981;
'Run Like Hell' edited from performances on 14, 15, and 17 June 1981;
'Mother', 'Hey You' and 'The Show Must Go On', 16 June 1981;
'Goodbye Blue Sky', 17 June 1981.

In addition, 'Another Brick in the Wall, Part 2', 'Comfortably Numb', and 'Run Like Hell' were performed at all of Pink Floyd's 1987–1989 shows. Live versions of these songs, recorded at Nassau Coliseum between 19 and 23 August 1988, are available on *Delicate Sound of Thunder* (22 November 1988). A live version of 'Run Like Hell', recorded at the Omni in Atlanta on 5 November 1987, is available on the *On the Turning Away CD* single (24 November 1987). Further live versions of 'Comfortably Numb' and 'Run Like Hell', recorded at Knebworth Park on 30 June 1990, are available on *Knebworth: The Album* (6 August 1990)

'Another Brick in the Wall, Part 2', 'Comfortably Numb', and 'Run Like Hell' were included in each of the 1994 tour dates. Live versions of these songs from the band's run of dates at Earls Court, London in October 1994 are available on *P•U•L•S•E* (29 May 1995). 'Hey You' (not included on *P•U•L•S•E*) was performed as the first encore on most dates of *The Division Bell* tour in 1994.

Reviews

> The tale of [a] rock star makes it; falls apart; is put together to perform by those whose lives depend on him; goes bonkers, turns fascist and faces retribution. Its themes of loneliness, war, loveless marriages and overbearing mothers struck an enormous chord with audiences the world over. Despite some of the morbidity of most of the material, there are some very beautiful tunes nestling amid the pomp, most notably the David Gilmour co-write, 'Comfortably Numb', with Bob Ezrin's orchestration and Gilmour's searing guitar solo. It has become the single track that most defines Pink Floyd.
>
> Daryl Easlea, BBC Music (2007)

> Long-time Pink Floyd fans will find the requisite number of bone-crushing riffs and Saturn-bound guitar screams ('In the Flesh'), along with one of the loveliest ballads the band has ever recorded ('Comfortably Numb'). And the singing throughout is—at last—truly first-rate, clear, impassioned. While *The Wall*'s length is certainly justified by the breadth of its thematic concerns, the music is stretched a bit thin. Even Floyd starved devotees may not be sucked into *The Wall*'s relatively flat aural ambiance on first hearing. But when they finally are—and then get a good look at that forbidding lyrical landscape—they may wonder which way is out real fast.
>
> Kurt Loder, *Rolling Stone* (February 1980)

The Final Cut (1983)

Recorded July–December 1982 at Gilmour's home studio at Hookend Manor, Waters' Billiard Room Studios at East Sheen, Mayfair Studios, Olympic Studios, EMI Studios (Abbey Road), Eel Pie Studios, Audio International, and RAK Studios. Produced by Roger Waters, David Gilmour, Michael Kamen, and James Guthrie. First released 21 March 1983 (UK: Harvest SHPF 1983); 2 April 1983 (US: Columbia QC 38243).

> By *The Final Cut*, I'd grown too weary of fighting to assert my musical judgement.
>
> David Gilmour, interview with Mark Blake (2008)

Whilst hardly the most uplifting listen, there is much to enjoy and even more to admire in the last Pink Floyd album to feature Roger Waters. It's Waters' *de facto* debut solo album, and, lyrically, may well be his finest hour. In the final analysis, if the previous four Pink Floyd albums, from *The Dark Side of the Moon* through to *The Wall*, are their collective definitive statements, then *The Final Cut* is Waters'. Furthermore, despite the friction and dissent that plagued these sessions, David Gilmour provides some of his best-regarded guitar solos. It is not really a Pink Floyd album, but it is still more than rather good.

The album has a convoluted history. Originally conceived as either an expanded soundtrack to the film of *The Wall*, or a collection of leftovers from that project ('*Spare Bricks*') it morphed into something different: an album as powerful as *The Wall,* but much, much more personal to its creator. The record weaves two themes—Waters' grief for his father, killed at Anzio in 1944; and his fury at modern leaders' betrayal of past sacrifices by making political capital out of conflicts like the Falklands War.

> [*The Final Cut*] was about how, in the aftermath of the Second World War and the Attlee government and the introduction of the Welfare State, we felt we were moving forward into something resembling some kind of Utopian dream of a liberal country where we would all look after one another and slowly that dream had become eroded. There's a selfishness in us and a lack of community spirit that led us, by the 80s into a doctrine of a pragmatic, radical, Reaganite-Thatcherite economic system. That's the system of values to which, by and large, we still cling.
>
> Roger Waters, *Mojo* (March 2003)

Four of the 'new' songs were recycled from demos made for *The Wall*. 'Your Possible Pasts', 'One of the Few', 'The Hero's Return', and, somewhat surprisingly, the magnificent title track. David Gilmour offered no new songs for the album, meaning that, between the song 'Wish You Were Here', written in early 1975, and his credits on *A Momentary Lapse of Reason*, released in September 1987, he contributed just four co-writes for Pink Floyd.

The Final Cut was recorded with a clutch of session musicians over several months in eight different studios. Nick Mason was not needed once his drums tracks were completed: on one track he was replaced with UK-domiciled American drummer Andy Newmark.[14] The departed Rick Wright was replaced by Michael Kamen and Andy Bown. As sessions progressed and tensions built, Waters and Gilmour elected to work separately. The final result is dominated by Roger Waters with an elegance, beauty, and anger that is quite unlike anything else in their catalogue.

> *The Final Cut* was absolutely misery to make, although I listened to it of late and I rather like a lot of it. You can hear the mad tension running through it all.
>
> Roger Waters, interviewed by Chris Salewicz (June 1987)

This album does not contain music to share with friends. It demands a darkened room, headphones, and forty-three minutes of rapt attention. With only four guitar solos, no songs with verse-chorus-verse structure, a knotty subject matter, and Waters' almost unrelenting whine throughout, *The Final Cut* is, as Mark Blake writes, 'not entry-level Floyd for the curious'.[15] However, like Waters himself, his last album with Pink Floyd has aged with surprising grace.[16]

> Waters' fixity of vision gives this album a claustrophobic intensity, a character all of its own—a peculiarly English blend of bitterness.
>
> Toby Manning, *The Rough Guide to Pink Floyd* (2006)

> Making *The Final Cut* was the final straw. I was virtually the only one in the studio and the others just didn't seem to care. Dave wanted me to wait until he had written some more material, but given that he'd written maybe three songs in the whole of the previous five years I couldn't see when that was going to happen. It all got very nasty. The name Pink Floyd should have died then, but in the long run I don't suppose it really matters.
>
> Roger Waters interviewed by Johnny Black, *Mojo* (March 2003)

None of the songs from *The Final Cut* have been performed in concert by Pink Floyd. Roger Waters has included several in his solo tours however: 'The Gunner's Dream' (1984–1985, 2006), 'Not Now John' (1987), 'Get Your Filthy Hands Off My Desert' (1999–2002), 'Southampton Dock' (1999–2002, 2006–2008), and 'The Fletcher Memorial Home' (2006–2008).

'The Post War Dream'

Roger Waters: lyrics, music, vocals, bass
David Gilmour: guitar
Nick Mason: drums
Michael Kamen: harmonium

An overture to the album, with sound effects (a radio tuning *à la* 'Wish You Were Here'), a quiet opening section, and a muscular, more melodramatic ending, 'The Post War Dream' lays down the album's concept from the outset. The line 'If it wasn't for the nips being so good at building ships the yards would still be open on the Clyde / And it can't be much fun for them beneath the rising sun with all their kids committing suicide' is a direct reference to a contract for replacing a ship lost in the Falklands conflict that was awarded to Japan.

So, *The Final Cut*. A concept album about the state of Great Britain in the post-Falklands 1980s, triggered by the senselessness of that conflict and a lingering bitterness of the lack of social progress in the years after the sacrifice of millions in the Second World War, Waters' father included.

This is a both a political and deeply personal album.

'Your Possible Pasts'

Roger Waters: lyrics, music, bass, guitar, vocals
David Gilmour: guitar
Nick Mason: drums
Michael Kamen: electric piano
Andy Bown: Hammond organ
Ray Cooper: percussion

One of the leftover songs from *The Wall*, some of the lyrics of the chorus were used in the film *Pink Floyd—The Wall*, where the lines were read by the main character, Pink, in-between the songs 'Waiting for the Worms' and 'Stop'.

With shifting dynamics and a superb guitar solo by David Gilmour, 'Your Possible Pasts' is 'a titanic blend of stadium rock, psychedelia and pathos, concluding with devastating imagery'.[17]

'One of the Few'

Roger Waters: lyrics, music, vocals, acoustic guitar, synthesiser

One of the songs destined for *Spare Bricks*, this short, acoustic, linking track bridges the louder, heavier 'Your Possible Pasts' and 'The Hero's Return'. Its musical theme is repeated in 'Not Now John'.

'The Hero's Return'

Roger Waters: lyrics, music, vocals, bass, synthesiser, guitar
David Gilmour: guitar
Nick Mason: drums, percussion
Andy Bown: electric piano

Demoed for *The Wall* with the title 'Teacher, Teacher' and almost entirely rewritten for *Spare Bricks*, 'The Hero's Return' is a tightly arranged up-tempo track with layers of acoustic and electric guitars.

It was released as the B-side to 'Not Now John', featuring an extra verse that was not on the album version.

> Jesus Christ, I might as well be dead / I can't see how dangerous it must feel to me / Training human cogs for the machine / Without some shell-shocked lunatic like me / Bombarding their still soft shells with sticks and stones that were lying around / In the pile of unspeakable feelings I'd found / When I turned back the stone / Turned over the stone / Of my own disappointment back home

'The Gunner's Dream'

Roger Waters: lyrics, music, vocals, bass
David Gilmour: guitar
Nick Mason: drums
Raphael Ravenscroft: saxophone
Michael Kamen: piano, electric piano
Andy Bown: piano
The National Philharmonic Orchestra, conducted and arranged by Michael Kamen

> The centrepiece of the album is 'The Gunner's Dream'. Waters' voice is beautifully matched to words whose understatement adds to the power. Phrases like, 'Floating down through the skies, memories come rushing up to meet me now of a place between the heavens and the corner of some foreign field' are impressively restrained. Indeed, both the music and words hook into an English elegiac tradition. As with Floyd's one time collaborator Roy Harper and that other English maverick Richard Thompson there is simultaneously a fragile nostalgia and barely disguised anger.
>
> Rachel Mann, *The Quietus* (June 2013)

'The Gunner's Dream' tells the story and thoughts of an airman as he falls to his death during a raid. He dreams of a safe world in a future without war. Some of Roger Waters' very best lyrics, with some dazzling imagery ('the silver in her hair shines in the cold

November air'), the song is lifted further by a crisp production and a tremendous saxophone solo by Raphael Ravenscroft.

The line about maniacs 'blow[ing] holes in bandsmen by remote control' is a reference to an IRA bomb that exploded underneath a bandstand in Regent's Park London on 20 July 1982, killing seven British servicemen.

'Paranoid Eyes'

Roger Waters: lyrics, music, vocals, bass, and guitar
Nick Mason: drums
Michael Kamen: piano
Andy Bown: organ
Ray Cooper: percussion
The National Philharmonic Orchestra, conducted and arranged by Michael Kamen

Employing Roger Waters' favourite G to Cadd9 chord progression (see 'Pigs on the Wing' or 'Mother'), what starts as a simple reworking of 'Nobody Home' becomes a touching eulogy for the British way of life. There is no angst-ridden bark here, as Waters employs his much warmer register. 'Paranoid Eyes' is an utterly sincere and ultimately very moving song.

'Get Your Filthy Hands off My Desert'

Roger Waters: lyrics, music, vocals, guitar
The National Philharmonic Orchestra, conducted and arranged by Michael Kamen

A lively string quartet belies extreme criticism of British Prime Minister Margaret Thatcher. The line 'Maggie, over lunch one day, took a cruiser with all hands' references the sinking of the Argentine cruiser *General Belgrano* by the British Navy on 2 May 1982. The sinking of *General Belgrano* was highly controversial in both the United Kingdom and Argentina at the time, and remains so to this day.

'The Fletcher Memorial Home'

Roger Waters: lyrics, music, vocals, bass
David Gilmour: guitar
Nick Mason: drums
Michael Kamen: piano
The National Philharmonic Orchestra, conducted and arranged by Michael Kamen

In this magnificent song, Waters calls out the world leaders of the early '80s—including Margaret Thatcher, Ronald Reagan, Leonid Brezhnev, and others—and invites them to a retirement home for 'incurable tyrants and kings'. With outstanding lyrics that are simultaneously sarcastic and melodramatic, 'The Fletcher Memorial Home' was sensibly included in the band's 2001 best-of album, quite at home nestling between 'Time' and 'Comfortably Numb'.

> It dates from one of the worst periods of my life. It was a nightmare working with Roger at that time and I'm heavily disinclined to listen to *The Final Cut* or anything to do with it. But it's a great song.
>
> David Gilmour, *Mojo* (October 2001)

'Southampton Dock'

Roger Waters: lyrics, music, guitar, bass, vocals
Michael Kamen: piano
The National Philharmonic Orchestra, conducted and arranged by Michael Kamen

A simple Dylan-esque folk ballad with a carefully constructed and picturesque lyric. Waters links his overriding anti-war theme of the first half of the album to the sight of British soldiers heading to the Falklands in 1982.

'The Final Cut'

Roger Waters: lyrics, music, vocals, bass
David Gilmour: guitar
Nick Mason: drums
Michael Kamen: piano, harmonium
The National Philharmonic Orchestra conducted and arranged by Michael Kamen

The best Pink Floyd songs are built on shifting dynamics—either a slow build towards release or a constantly changing pattern of loud and quiet passages: 'Careful with That Axe, Eugene'; 'Echoes'; 'Atom Heart Mother'; 'Us and Them'; 'Shine on You Crazy Diamond'; and 'Hey You'.

Like these, 'The Final Cut' employs potent dynamics and some of Waters' most poetic imagery to produce one of Pink Floyd's most powerful songs, dealing, as it does, with isolation, repression and an inability to connect with the world at large.

Waters has never really been credited for his sense of humour.[18] Yet we see glimpses of black comedy amongst the vulnerability, where Waters employs a series of metaphors in getting to the heart of his psyche: successfully get past the mines, dogs, CCTV, weapons, and security measures and he might let you in. If he is at home, that is.

David Gilmour, whose presence is otherwise negligible on this album, plays a sublime guitar solo on this title track. It is as expressive a solo as he has ever recorded—

mournful, tuneful, and angry at the same time, adding some much-needed melodic variety to the often one-note compositions on this album.

All in all, an astounding song.

'Not Now John'

Roger Waters: lyrics, music, vocals, bass, guitar, synthesiser
David Gilmour: vocals, guitar
Nick Mason: drums
Andy Bown: Hammond organ

Something of an anomaly on this album, a cuckoo in the nest—an up-tempo almost-rocker, the only track with lead vocals by David Gilmour. The message, though, relates to the rest of the album: society's ignorance of political and economic problems, and the common man not being able to see further than the end of his nose.

It was released as a single on 3 May 1983, suitably bowdlerised, and reached No. 30 in the UK.

'Two Suns in the Sunset'

Roger Waters: lyrics, music, bass, vocals, guitar
David Gilmour: guitar
Andy Newmark: drums
Andy Bown: Hammond organ
Raphael Ravenscroft: saxophone
Michael Kamen: piano

Surely the most downbeat finale of any album—what would be the final result of a world obsessed with war and control? Nuclear holocaust and global annihilation, delivered with a chilling and a humbling final lyric: 'Ashes and diamonds / Foe and friend / We were all equal in the end'

Listen closely for the weather report at the end: 'Tomorrow will be cloudy with scattered showers spreading from the east with an expected high of 4000 degrees Celsius'

With a tricky time signature (a mixture of 9/8, 4/4, 7/8, and 3/8), Nick Mason deferred drumming duties to session-musician Andy Newmark on this track.[19]

So, with that, we say farewell to the Roger Waters era of Pink Floyd. The band would never sound this vital again.

> We'd been arguing since 1974, for God's sake. Too long. At a certain point you have to say, this is not working, the point has come to break up.
>
> Roger Waters, *Mojo* (December 1999)

Bonus Track: 'When the Tigers Broke Free'

Written by Roger Waters.

Released as a single on 26 July 1982.

Waters relates his feelings when he learned the truth about his father's death at Anzio during the Italian Campaign of the Second World War; hardly hit-single material, but a surprise Top 40 hit in the UK.

Reviews

> If Floyd had famously been falling apart for years, under stress from the conflicting egos of Waters and Gilmour, it's not unreasonable to suggest that *The Final Cut* is, from the title down, the ultimate public statement of a band's collapse into self-indulgence and failure. It is certainly a candidate for most depressing album of the '80s.
>
> Rachel Mann, *The Quietus* (June 2013)

> This may be art rock's crowning masterpiece, but it is also something more. With *The Final Cut*, Pink Floyd caps its career in classic form. The result is essentially a Roger Waters solo album and it's a superlative achievement on several levels.
>
> Kurt Loder, *Rolling Stone* (April 1983)

5

Floyd Phase 5: 1986–2014 The Music Played and Played

A Momentary Lapse of Reason (1987)

Recorded October 1986–May 1987, at the Astoria, Richmond-upon-Thames; Mayfair Studios, London; Audio International Studios, London; A&M Studios, Los Angeles. Produced by David Gilmour and Bob Ezrin. First released 7 September 1987 (UK: EMI, EMD 1003; US: Columbia, OC 40599).

In which David Gilmour gets more solo writing credits than the rest of his Pink Floyd career put together.

The 1980s were not kind to many of the classic rock artists of the 1970s. Overuse of technology and lashings of reverb make many albums of the 1980s simply unlistenable, this album included.[1] The back-to-basics concept of *MTV Unplugged*, first broadcast in November 1989, put the focus firmly back on songwriting craft and back-to-basics live performance, and for that we should be grateful. In the interim, we suffered the unhappy spectacle of baggy-suited and floppy-haired forty-something rockers, attempting to look and/or sound like Duran Duran.

> Recording *A Momentary Lapse of Reason* was a very, very difficult process. We were all sort of catatonic.
>
> David Gilmour interview in *Guitar World Presents Pink Floyd* (2002)

The spark of the creative process for the first album by Pink Floyd Mk. III was lit in July 1985, where David Gilmour performed at the London Live Aid concert as part of Bryan Ferry's band. Gilmour connected musically and socially with Ferry's keyboard player, Jon Carin, and they would subsequently jam together at Gilmour's home studio at Hookend Manor. Carin brought one of his own demos along and this formed the basis for the song 'Learning to Fly'. Other collaborators would follow, including Roxy Music's guitarist Phil Manzanera, 10CC's Eric Stewart, and lyricist Anthony Moore from the 70s bands Slapp Happy and Henry Cow.

By the time co-producer Bob Ezrin was recruited in summer 1986, Gilmour had most of a new album ready to roll. Initial sessions took place at Gilmour's houseboat on the Thames near Richmond, and at two studios in London.

Sessions moved to Los Angeles in February 1987 to avoid constant calls from Roger Waters' lawyers, and bassist Tony Levin was hired to provide a distinctly non-Waters bottom end. Other notable session musicians recruited in Los Angeles included saxophonists Scott Page, Tom Scott, and Supertramp's John Helliwell; drummers Carmine Appice and Jim Keltner; guitarist Michael Landau; and Little Feat's keyboard player Bill Payne.

The truth is that there were many better songs on Gilmour's 1984 solo album *About Face*. Pink Floyd were, at this stage, a one-man brand name with a famous repertoire. However, there is some wheat here. The two parts of 'A New Machine' are scintillating, and both 'On the Turning Away' and 'Sorrow' have magnificent (if overlong) guitar solos. 'Yet Another Movie' has also emerged unscathed from the production mire.

As an album, *A Momentary Lapse of Reason* worked as an advertisement for a huge world tour, where it would be performed in its entirety, note for note. While not a complete waste, *A Momentary Lapse of Reason* is hardly representative of Pink Floyd's best work. Their next album *The Division Bell* would be a marked improvement.

As Mark Blake writes, '*A Momentary Lapse of Reason* was the right album for the times. Where it falls down is that it is stuck in that time.'

> I was slightly angry that they managed to get away with it. I was bemused and a bit disappointed that the 'Great Unwashed' couldn't tell the fucking difference. Well, actually they can. I'm being unkind. There are a huge number of people who can tell the difference, but there were also a large number of people who couldn't.
>
> Roger Waters interviewed by John Harris, *Mojo* (November 2004)

> There are some lovely moments on it—'Sorrow', 'On the Turning Away', 'Learning to Fly'. But, like most people, we got trapped in this '80s thing.
>
> David Gilmour, interview with Mark Blake (2008)

'Signs of Life'

David Gilmour: music, guitars, synths
Nick Mason: vocal recitation
Richard Wright: Kurzweil synthesiser
Tony Levin: bass guitar
Jon Carin: synthesiser
Bob Ezrin: music

> Out of the speakers came a big, lumbering groove with a rather lovely guitar figure on it.
>
> Guy Pratt, *My Bass and Other Animals* (2007)

What starts as a promising overture to the first new Pink Floyd music for four years, and only their third album in the previous ten, proves to be a false dawn. The playing is crystalline and the mood is foreboding and everything is all pleasant and promising, but it ultimately does not go anywhere.

'Learning to Fly'

David Gilmour: lyrics, music, vocals, guitars
Nick Mason: drums
Richard Wright: keyboards, vocals
Jon Carin: music, keyboards
Steve Forman: percussion
Tony Levin: bass
Darlene Koldenhaven: backing vocals
Carmen Twillie: backing vocals
Phyllis St. James: backing vocals
Donnie Gerrard: backing vocals
Bob Ezrin: music
Anthony Moore: lyrics

The first sights and sounds of the new-look Pink Floyd. What is this noisy, clattering nonsense? 'Learning to Fly' is based on a demo by new keyboard honcho Jon Carin with musical assistance from co-producer Bob Ezrin, and lyrical support from Anthony Moore.

'Learning to Fly', despite (or perhaps because of) its distinctly non-Floyd sound, would be the biggest hit from the record. Both Gilmour and Mason had been taking flying lessons, and many of Gilmour's lyrics voice the feelings of the freedom that flight gave him. Gilmour later admitted later that there was a double meaning, and it was also about starting fresh as the new leader of the band after Waters' departure.

Released as a single, slightly edited, on 15 September 1987.

'The Dogs of War'

David Gilmour: lyrics, music, guitar, vocals
Tony Levin: bass
Scott Page: saxophone
Tom Scott: saxophone
Carmine Appice: drums, percussion
Jon Carin: keyboards

Bill Payne: organ
Darlene Koldenhaven: backing vocals
Carmen Twillie: backing vocals
Phyllis St. James: backing vocals
Donnie Gerrard: backing vocals
Anthony Moore: lyrics

'Dogs of War' trudges through six minutes of vague, ugly protest in a slow 12/8, with a momentary uplifting 4/4 section during the saxophone solo. Neither Nick Mason nor Richard Wright perform on this song.

> I came home one day and there was a message on my machine from Bob Ezrin. He said, 'Hey Carmine, I'm in the studio with Pink Floyd and there's a track that's just screaming for some Carmine fills.' I called him back, I said, 'Where's Nick Mason?' He said, 'He's here, but he's a bit rusty and everybody wants a bit of a change, so they're bringing in guest drummers.' All I did was fill up a 24-track with drum parts and they edited it all together.
>
> Carmine Appice, quoted in *songfacts.com*

Voted 'the worst ever Pink Floyd' song in *The Amazing Pudding*'s 1989 readers' poll.

'One Slip'

David Gilmour: lyrics, music, guitar, vocals
Nick Mason: drums, percussion
Richard Wright: keyboards
Jim Keltner: drums
Tony Levin: Chapman Stick
Jon Carin: keyboards
Bob Ezrin: keyboards
Michael Landau: guitar
Darlene Koldenhaven: backing vocals
Carmen Twillie: backing vocals
Phyllis St. James: backing vocals
Donnie Gerrard: backing vocals
Phil Manzanera: co-composition

Released as single on 3 October 1987.[2]

Opening with a re-working of the sound effects and tom-toms from 'Time' and Gilmour's trademark reverb-laden 'chucka-chucka' guitar sound, this very commercial song is typical late-80s stadium rock fare, sounding nothing at all like Pink Floyd.

The slippery bass solo in the middle is performed by ex- and future King Crimson bassist Tony Levin on a Chapman stick. Notably, Levin had been chief bassist on ex-Genesis singer Peter Gabriel's massive 1986 success *So*, from which source this song takes much of its sound and feel.

> The alarms on the front was me with the alarm system at the studio. Strangely enough I had a friend who worked in another studio and they had exactly the same alarm system. And he said, 'Oh, God that sound! I can't believe you used that!'
>
> Andy Jackson, Pink Floyd's sound engineer, interviewed by Craig Bailey, December 2000

'On the Turning Away'

David Gilmour: lyrics, music, guitars, vocals, sequencers
Nick Mason: drums, percussion
Richard Wright: organ, backing vocals
Tony Levin: bass
Jim Keltner: drums
Jon Carin: synthesiser
Anthony Moore: lyrics

Starting as a slow, ethereal English folk ballad, ending with a mass guitar blow-out, the lyrics in this, one of the better songs on the album, are perhaps over-written. However, after the horrors of side one of this album, this track is a welcome relief.

> 'Turning Away' is about the political situations in the world. We have these rather right-wing conservative governments that don't seem to care about many things other than looking after themselves.
>
> David Gilmour (*Only Music*, December 1987)

With lyrics that echo the concerns of Roger Waters—the plight of the disadvantaged—Waters himself has said that there were 'one or two' pieces from *A Momentary Lapse of Reason* that he would have seen as belonging on a 'proper' Floyd album. He never admitted to which tracks he referred, but this is surely a candidate for one of them.

Released as a single worldwide in December 1987, it reached No. 55 in the UK singles chart. Pink Floyd fans with open minds are directed to Richie Havens' astoundingly powerful cover version from his album *Wishing Well* (2002).

'Yet Another Movie'

David Gilmour: lyrics, music, guitar, vocals, programming, sequencer
Nick Mason: drums
Patrick Leonard: music, synthesisers
Tony Levin: bass
Jim Keltner: drums
Steve Forman: percussion

Something of a surprise this one. Despite lots of '80s synths and drum sounds, the dream-like 'Yet Another Movie' has a lovely deep production, some exquisite wriggly bass from Tony Levin, and a guitar solo with some real intent. If only the whole album had been this good. The extended, melancholic coda started life as one of a trio of demos apparently rejected by Roger Waters for *The Final Cut*.

'Round and Around'

David Gilmour: music, guitar
Jon Carin: keyboards
Tony Levin: bass

'Round and Around' is a short 5/8 instrumental coda to 'Yet Another Movie'.

'A New Machine (Part 1)'

David Gilmour: lyrics, music, vocals, vocoder, programming, synthesiser
Patrick Leonard: synthesiser

'A New Machine' features Gilmour's heavily processed and distorted vocals, weary and questioning with wide-open spaces in between each phrase. It is quite unlike anything else Pink Floyd has done, before or after, and, after thirty years, this track still jumps out from the other rather backward-looking, over-produced songs heard elsewhere on this album.

'Terminal Frost'

David Gilmour: music, guitar
Nick Mason: drum machine
Richard Wright: piano, Kurzweil synthesiser
Jon Carin: keyboards
Tom Scott: saxophones
John Helliwell: saxophones
Bob Ezrin: percussion

Question: What's the difference between a drum machine and a drummer? Answer: You only need to punch the arrangement into a drum machine once.

'Terminal Frost' is the longest and least interesting instrumental on the album. Nick Mason relegates himself to programming rather than playing the drums, and Gilmour's solo is clichéd and dull—the band even released a 'do your own solo' version with the guitar removed as the B-side of 'Learning to Fly'. Musically and technically competent, but with absolutely no soul, not even howling saxophone from Tom Scott and John Helliwell can lift this above insipid rocky muzak.

'A New Machine (Part 2)'

David Gilmour: lyrics, music, vocals, vocoder, programming, synthesiser
Patrick Leonard: synthesiser

A brief continuation of Part 1. Worth it.

> 'A New Machine' has a sound I've never heard anyone do. The noise gates, the Vocoders, opened up something new which to me seemed like a wonderful sound effect that no one had done before; it's innovation of a sort.
>
> David Gilmour, *Musician*, 1992

'Sorrow'

David Gilmour: lyrics, music, guitar, vocals, keyboards, programming, synthesiser, drum machine
Richard Wright: Kurzweil synthesiser
Tony Levin: bass
Bob Ezrin: keyboards
Darlene Koldenhaven: backing vocals
Carmen Twillie: backing vocals
Phyllis St. James: backing vocals
Donnie Gerard: backing vocals

> Everything about this song is absolutely fucking enormous.
>
> Guy Pratt, *My Bass and Other Animals* (2007)

'Sorrow' is focused and positive, probably the strongest song on the album. A truly massive guitar sound and a horrible tinny drum machine mark this song out as pure 1987. However, under the rock-bluster there is a smartly produced track with, finally, some of the old Pink Floyd dynamics. We also have one of Gilmour's best opening lines ('the sweet smell of a great sorrow lies over the land') as well as some of his worst ('his blood has frozen and curdled with fright / his knees have trembled and given way in the night'). The lyric includes the phrase 'louder than words', later to be re-used as the title of Pink Floyd's last-ever song. Shame about the drum machine.

Live Performances

'Signs of Life', 'Learning to Fly', 'Dogs of War', 'On the Turning Away', 'Yet Another Movie', 'Round and Around', and 'Sorrow' were performed at every full concert on the tour to promote *A Momentary Lapse of Reason* in 1987–1989. 'One Slip' was performed at most of the dates on this same tour, always as the first encore as the crowd waited to hear 'Comfortably Numb'. 'A New Machine' and 'Terminal Frost' were often added to the set list as well. Two songs recorded early in tour were released on contemporary CD singles and are unavailable elsewhere. 'On the Turning Away' can be heard on the *On the Turning Away* CD and 12-inch singles (24 November 1987), and 'Dogs of War' is on the *One Slip* CD single (June 1988); both were recorded at the Omni in Atlanta on 5 November 1987. Live versions of 'Learning to Fly', 'Dogs of War', 'On the Turning Away', 'Yet Another Movie', 'Round and Around' and 'Sorrow', all recorded at Nassau Coliseum between 19–23 August 1988, are available on *Delicate Sound of Thunder* (22 November 1988).

'Learning to Fly' and 'Sorrow' were performed at every date on the 1994 tour for *The Division Bell*. 'On the Turning Away' was added to the set list whenever the full *Dark Side of the Moon* album was not played. Live versions of 'Learning to Fly' and 'Sorrow' are available on *P•U•L•S•E* (released 29 May 1995, recorded 14 October 1994 and 20 September 1994 respectively).

Reviews

> A David Gilmour solo album in all but name, heavily featuring the kind of atmospheric instrumental music and Gilmour guitar sound typical of the Floyd before the now-departed Roger Waters took over, but lacking Waters' unifying vision and lyrical ability.
>
> *AllMusic Review* by William Ruhlmann

> When I say Pink Floyd, what do you think of? *The Dark Side of the Moon*? *The Wall*? Roger Waters? LSD? Certainly not *A Momentary Lapse of Reason*. At least I hope. Is it the worst album ever written? No. Does it live up to Pink Floyd's reputation? No. But, this album shows you, despite all of Roger Waters' quirky obsessions and his control freak ego, he was Pink Floyd.
>
> Porter W. Richards, *Sputnik Music* (September 2007)

> [*A Momentary Lapse of Reason*] makes for a frustrating listen because buried behind the long intros and unnecessary sound effects is the foundation of what could be a good record.
>
> Cory Garcia, *Houston Press* (2012)

The Division Bell (1994)

Recorded January–December 1993 at Britannia Row Studios; the Astoria, Richmond-upon-Thames; Abbey Road Studios, Metropolis Studios and The Creek Recording Studios, London. Produced by Bob Ezrin and David Gilmour. First released 28 March 1994 (UK: 7243 8 28984 2 9, CD EMD 1055; US: Columbia CK 64200).

> And then when the second one came out…well, it had got totally Spinal Tap by then. Lyrics went written by the new wife. Well, they are! I mean, give me a fucking break! Come on. And what a nerve to call that Pink Floyd. It was an awful record.
>
> Roger Waters interviewed by John Harris, *Mojo* (November 2004)

Although a big seller on its release in 1994 and the band's fourth UK Number One album, time has not been kind to many of the tracks on *The Division Bell*. Containing one *bona fide* classic in 'High Hopes', only three other songs—'Marooned', 'What Do You Want from Me?', and 'A Great Day for Freedom'—rise above the remaining stodgy stadium rock. Richard Wright's 'Wearing the Inside Out' provides a welcome change of pace, but provides short respite from the Floyd-lite which dominates this disappointing album.

Even its vague concept—the concept of communication as a great but limited tool—is recycled from *Wish You Were Here*. The many thinly-veiled references to Roger Waters are merely wearisome.

The album's genesis was in early 1993 when Gilmour, Mason and the now-once-again-full-member Wright convened at Britannia Row for writing sessions. Gilmour would record their jam sessions and, years later, many of these recordings would form the basis of the very last Pink Floyd album.

'Cluster One'

David Gilmour: music, guitars
Nick Mason: drums, percussion
Richard Wright: music, piano, Kurzweil synthesisers

As with *A Momentary Lapse of Reason*, Pink Floyd's new album starts with sound effects and an instrumental. 'Cluster One' is pleasant enough, if hardly ground-breaking in approach.

> When we first started collecting the jam material together we divided it up into three categories, which were acoustic, blues and cosmic. And bits we glued together we called clusters. And the instrumentals, because they never had any reason to take on a new title, they just stayed with their old titles for a long time. 'Cluster One' was always 'Cluster One' and it just stuck. Bob Ezrin, posted a note on the message board on the Net or CompuServe saying 'Anybody got any space noises?' And somebody wrote back! This guy who goes and stands on the top of Mount Washington, I think, in thunder storms holding this great big metal antennae! Recording the electromagnetic stuff! And it is the sound of electromagnetic noise from the solar wind. I mean, it just sounds like a lot of crackles to me and you. But that's what it is.
>
> Andy Jackson, Pink Floyd's sound engineer, interviewed by Craig Bailey, December 2000

According to Vernon Fitch the song was listed as 'Nearly Touching/Cluster One' in a February 1994 press release.[3]

'What Do You Want from Me?'

David Gilmour: lyrics, music, guitars, vocals
Richard Wright: music, Hammond organ, synthesisers, electric piano, vocals
Nick Mason: drums, percussion
Jon Carin: keyboards
Guy Pratt: bass guitar
Sam Brown: backing vocals
Durga McBroom: backing vocals
Carol Kenyon: backing vocals
Polly Samson: lyrics

A great wallop of a blues song given a much harder edge in concert, with Gilmour really grunting out the vocals, 'What Do You Want from Me?' was a mainstay of the 1994 tour promoting *The Division Bell*. The lyric appears to directly confront the band's audience, an unusual subject matter for the usually easy-going Gilmour

> Should I sing until I can't sing any more? / Play these strings until my fingers are raw? / You're so hard to please / What do you want from me?

Gilmour revisited the song on his 2016 solo tours.

> Only on What Do You Want from Me[?] does Gilmour sound like he cares.
>
> Tom Graves, *Rolling Stone* (16 June 1994)

'Poles Apart'

David Gilmour: lyrics, music, guitars, bass, vocals
Nick Mason: drums, percussion
Richard Wright: keyboards
Jon Carin: programming
Polly Samson: lyrics
Nick Laird-Clowes: lyrics

An open letter in an open tuning to both Syd Barrett ('you were always the golden boy') and Roger Waters ('hey you, did you ever realise what you'd become?'). In places the music is reminiscent of the central section of 'Dogs', even reprising that track's droning 'dragged down by the stone' as 'and did you know?'

Overall, though, 'Poles Apart' lacks the bite and bark of 'Dogs', and loses momentum halfway through when the main composition is deconstructed to oom-pah synthesisers and sound effects.

'Marooned'

David Gilmour: music, guitars
Richard Wright: music, Kurzweil synthesisers, piano
Nick Mason: drums, percussion
Jon Carin: keyboards
Guy Pratt: bass

A quite beautiful guitar-led instrumental based on a Richard Wright chord sequence which still sounds fabulous today; Gilmour's control, tone, pitch, and technique are remarkable, and Wright's piano chording underpins the entire piece. Despite the polite, pedestrian drumming, this could easily fit into *The Dark Side of the Moon*: an 'Any Colour You Like' for the 1990s.

> I probably took three or four passes at it and took the best bits out of each.
>
> David Gilmour interview in *Guitar World Presents Pink Floyd* (2002)

Working titles were: 'Cosmic 13', 'The Whale Song', and 'The Whale Piece'. It was the winner of the 1995 Grammy for Best Rock Instrumental Performance.

'A Great Day for Freedom'

David Gilmour: lyrics, music, guitar, vocals
Richard Wright: piano

Nick Mason: drums, percussion
Guy Pratt: bass guitar
Jon Carin: programming
Polly Samson: lyrics

Gilmour injects some much-needed passion into *The Division Bell*. 'A Great Day for Freedom' addresses the hope of change following the fall of the Berlin Wall and the disappointment that followed.

> There was a wonderful moment of optimism when the Wall came down—the release of Eastern Europe from the non-democratic side of the socialist system. But what they have now doesn't seem to be much better. Again, I'm fairly pessimistic about it all. I sort of wish and live in hope, but I tend to think that history moves at a much slower pace than we think it does. I feel that real change takes a long, long time.
>
> David Gilmour interview in *Guitar World Presents Pink Floyd* (2002)

'Wearing the Inside Out'

Richard Wright: music, keyboards, vocals
David Gilmour: guitar, vocals, bass
Nick Mason: drums, percussion
Dick Parry: tenor saxophone
Sam Brown: backing vocals
Durga McBroom: backing vocals
Carol Kenyon: backing vocals
Anthony Moore: lyrics

A dark, atmospheric, and hauntingly vulnerable Richard Wright song: his first Pink Floyd lead vocal since 1973. It provides a significant change of feeling and timbre, reminding us just how important Wright was to the 'classic' Pink Floyd albums of the 1970s. Dick Parry, the sax player on the original recordings of 'Money', 'Us and Them' and 'Shine On You Crazy Diamond', really stands out on this almost return-to-form.

The LP version is different from the CD version, with a slight change in the lyrics: the first lines of the second verse ('I murmured a vow ... when I think aloud') were added to the first verse and the rest of the second verse ('Extinguished by the light with an empty smile') was left out, so that the LP version has a longer first verse and no second verse between 'This bleeding heart's not beating much' and 'I'm creeping back to life'.

The song had the working title 'Evrika', a hotel complex on the Black Sea. It was never performed live by Pink Floyd, but was sung by Richard Wright on the David Gilmour's 2006 tour for *On An Island*.

Another much better Wright/Moore song 'Breakthrough' would be a stand-out track on Wright's 1996 solo album *Broken China* and was a notable highlight of the Festival Hall concert that Gilmour and Wright performed together in 2002. What a shame it was not ready for *The Division Bell*, as it would have been a contender for one of the best latter-day Pink Floyd songs.

'Take It Back'

David Gilmour: lyrics, music, guitars, vocals
Richard Wright: keyboards
Nick Mason: drums, percussion
Tim Renwick: guitar
Jon Carin: programming
Guy Pratt: bass
Sam Brown: backing vocals
Durga McBroom: backing vocals
Carol Kenyon: backing vocals
Polly Samson: lyrics
Nick Laird-Clowes: lyrics
Bob Ezrin: music

Released as a single worldwide on 16 May 1994. It took four writers to create this, the most commercial song from *The Division Bell*, and therefore was a safe bet for the first single to be taken from the album. It sounds a lot like U2.

> 'Take It Back' would have fitted better on *A Momentary Lapse of Reason*, or even Gilmour's solo album *About Face*. Or neither.
>
> Mark Blake, *Pigs Might Fly: The Inside Story of Pink Floyd* (2007)

'Coming Back to Life'

David Gilmour: lyrics, music, vocals, guitar
Richard Wright: Kurzweil synthesisers, Hammond organ
Nick Mason: drums, percussion
Guy Pratt: bass
Jon Carin: keyboards

Some spikily tuneful guitar playing at the beginning of this solo Gilmour composition heralds a plodding song with not much inspiration on offer. Always something of a lumpy mid-tempo rocker when performed by Pink Floyd, the song gained a fresh, less-dense semi-acoustic arrangement in 2001 for the *David Gilmour in Concert* DVD.

'Keep Talking'

David Gilmour: lyrics, music, vocals, guitar
Richard Wright: music, Hammond organ, synthesiser
Nick Mason: drums, percussion
Tim Renwick: guitar
Gary Wallis: percussion
Jon Carin: programming, keyboards
Guy Pratt: bass
Bob Ezrin: percussion
Sam Brown: backing vocals
Durga McBroom: backing vocals
Carol Kenyon: backing vocals
Polly Samson: lyrics

One of the better songs on the album. Harking back to the sound of *Animals*, it uses backing vocals, a vicious guitar solo, and a sample of Stephen Hawking to maintain interest.

> I had a Zoom [effects box] in my control room one day and I was mucking about with something. Suddenly, I thought I should stick the E-bow on the strings and see what would happen. It sounded great, so we started writing a little duet for the E-bowed acoustic guitar and a keyboard. We never finished the piece, but Jon Carin decided to sample the E-bowed guitar part. We kept the sample and ended up using it as a loop on 'Take It Back' and again on 'Keep Talking'.
>
> David Gilmour interview in *Guitar World Presents Pink Floyd* (2002)

Released as a single worldwide on 17 October 1994, the single version has several edits, and is a much tighter arrangement than the track on the album.

'Lost for Words'

David Gilmour: lyrics, music, guitars, bass, vocals
Richard Wright: keyboards
Nick Mason: drums, percussion
Jon Carin: keyboards, programming
Polly Samson: lyrics

A pale rewrite of 'Wish You Were Here', with a very obvious swipe at Roger Waters.

> Even through the vagueness of the lyrics, one gets the feeling the band is firing broadsides at Waters. On 'Lost for Words', for example, David Gilmour sings: 'So I

open my door to my enemies/And I ask could we wipe the slate clean/But they tell me to please go fuck myself/You know you just can't win.' And so the war continues.

Tom Graves, *Rolling Stone* (16 June 1994)

In the middle of the song, there is a sound clip of a boxing match that was taken from the film *Champion* (1949), starring Kirk Douglas.

'High Hopes'

David Gilmour: lyrics, music, vocals, guitars, bass, lap steel guitar
Richard Wright: Kurzweil synthesisers
Nick Mason: drums, church bell, percussion
Jon Carin: piano
Polly Samson: lyrics

Released as a single worldwide on 17 October 1994.[4]

A eulogy to better times and happier places, 'High Hopes' evokes genuine feelings of sadness, reminiscence, and nostalgia, and can sit quite comfortably alongside any other Pink Floyd song in their long career together.

I think we made some of the Pink Floyd classics in our later incarnation. 'High Hopes' certainly falls into that category.

David Gilmour, interview with Mark Blake (2008)

The song was the first to be written for *The Division Bell.*

The song originated from a phrase that my girlfriend [co-writer Polly Samson] suggested, about how time brings you down. There was just something in it that sparked me into thinking about my childhood in Cambridge. [It] was much more personal than I've tended to be. And I suppose it set the scene for what was to follow.

David Gilmour interview in *Guitar World Presents Pink Floyd* (2002)

Gilmour's rich vocal tone evokes past personal glories and the passage of time, and that even in your fifties and beyond you can look to the future with high hopes.
It was as if the older, world-wearier voice of 'Fat Old Sun' had come back twenty-five years later to update the story.

Mark Blake, *Pigs Might Fly: The Inside Story of Pink Floyd* (2007)

The majestic closing section—Gilmour plays a fabulous lap steel solo that lifts and flies—is the highlight of post-Waters Pink Floyd.

Other Contemporary Pieces

'Soundscape'

This track consists of various ambient noises and is probably an extract of the (longer) tape that was played before the Floyd shows during *The Division Bell* tour. Somewhere in the middle, an extract of 'Cluster One' can be heard. Released on the cassette version of *P•U•L•S•E*.

Live Performances

'What Do You Want from Me?', 'A Great Day for Freedom', 'Take it Back', 'Keep Talking', 'Lost for Words', and 'High Hopes' were first performed at the opening night of the *Division Bell* tour at Joe Robbie Stadium, Miami, on 30 March 1994. 'What Do You Want from Me?' was a regular inclusion in the set, but dropped whenever the full *Dark Side of the Moon* album was performed. 'A Great Day for Freedom' was included in thirty-eight of the 112 concert dates in 1994. 'Take It Back' was included in all but one of the 1994 concert dates. 'Keep Talking' and 'High Hopes' were set list constants performed on every night of the tour, whereas 'Lost for Words' was included only a handful of times that year. Just once, on 4 September 1994, 'High Hopes' was played as part of the band's encore.

'Poles Apart' made its live debut at the Alamodome, San Antonio on 3 April 1994 and was performed another twenty-three times that year. 'Coming Back to Life' made its live debut at Texas Stadium, Irving on 29 April 1994, and was performed over forty times that year, at just under half of the shows on the tour. 'Marooned' was performed by Pink Floyd only twice: at Valle Hovin, Oslo, on 29 and 30 August 1994. [5]

Live versions available on *P•U•L•S•E* (29 May 1995) are 'Keep Talking', recorded in Hanover on 17 August 1994; 'What Do You Want from Me?', recorded in Rome on 21 September 1994; 'Coming Back to Life', recorded in London on 13 October 1994; 'High Hopes', edited from performances in London on 14, 19–21, and 29 October 1994; and 'A Great Day for Freedom', recorded in London on 19 October 1994.

Review

> *The Division Bell* is a quieter, more atmospheric and contemplative Pink Floyd, with lyrics so opaque and inert one cannot hope to plumb their meaning. The album gives off the uncomfortable whiff of middle-age and greying sensibilities.
>
> Tom Graves, *Rolling Stone* (16 June 1994)

The Endless River (2014)

Recorded at the Royal Albert Hall, London, 1968; Olympic Studios, London, 1993; Britannia Row Studios, London, 1993; the Astoria, Richmond-upon-Thames, 1993, 2013–2014 and Medina Studios, Hove, 2013–2014.

This album might sound great, but it has no heart and no soul. Compiled from a collection of outtakes from *The Division Bell*, with some overdubs in 2013 and 2014, *The Endless River* was a UK number one in 2014, and the most pre-ordered album of all time on Amazon. One wonders how many of the millions of copies sold were played more than once—this is surely the most disappointing release by any major music act of the last fifty years.[6]

> [*The Division Bell*] started off with two weeks with the three of them plus Guy Pratt on bass jamming. And I went down just to kind of hang out with them a couple of times. And, literally, they were just jamming and we just recorded the jams. Dave just had a machine out next to where he was playing and he just hit record if anything good was happening. And we just ended up with a big pile of tape of jams.
>
> Andy Jackson, Pink Floyd's sound engineer, interviewed by Craig Bailey, December 2000

'Things Left Unsaid'

David Gilmour: music, guitars
Richard Wright: music, keyboards
Nick Mason: percussion
Bob Ezrin: keyboards

> The spoken-word intro mumblings of 'Things Left Unsaid' simply reminding one that the comparable mutterings on *The Dark Side of the Moon* actually served a thematic purpose: here they're just window-dressing, luring fans into a desperately disappointing experience.
>
> Andy Gill, *The Independent* (5 November 2014)

The opening track of Pink Floyd's final album commences with sound effects, endlessly drawn-out keyboard chords, and dawn-of-time guitar. Sound familiar? 'Shine on You Crazy Diamond' this is not, no matter how hard it tries. It is not even as interesting as 'Signs of Life'.

'It's What We Do'

David Gilmour: music, guitars

Richard Wright: music, keyboards
Nick Mason: percussion

A suspense of glacial electronics and elegantly searing guitar.

David Fricke, *Rolling Stone* (7 November 2014)

More mid-'70s pastiche, this time with Mason's reliably pedestrian drum fills, a re-tread of the off-the-beat bass from 'Shine On You Crazy Diamond', keyboards from 'Welcome to the Machine', and a lead guitar performance taken straight from 'Marooned'. This would have provided a nice change of pace between some real songs, but here it just sounds leaden.

'Ebb and Flow'

David Gilmour: music, guitars
Richard Wright: music, keyboards
Nick Mason: percussion

A linking piece of shimmering electric piano and twiddly guitar, it ebbs and it flows. A chord change is the most interesting part.

'Sum'

David Gilmour: music, guitars
Richard Wright: music, keyboards
Nick Mason: music, percussion
Damon Iddins: keyboards

'Cluster One' revisited, until it morphs into 'One of These Days' with hints of 'Welcome to the Machine'. However, the sum of nothing is still nothing.

'Skins'

David Gilmour: music, guitars
Richard Wright: music, keyboards
Nick Mason: music, percussion
Andy Jackson: bass

'Skins' was the name of a drum riff used during *The Man and the Journey* in 1969. One can only assume that the barrel-scraping has reached that far back. It includes no melody whatsoever, and a re-tread of the wah-wah seagull noises from 'Echoes'.

'Unsung'

David Gilmour: guitars
Richard Wright: music, keyboards
Nick Mason: percussion

'Unsung' consists of bubbling sequencers, the octave-spanning guitar squalls from 'Marooned' and wide open piano chordings. It is short and insignificant, one of many tunes from *The Endless River* that sound like it is building up to something, but does not.

'Anisina'

David Gilmour: music, guitars
Richard Wright: keyboards
Nick Mason: percussion
Gilad Atzmon: tenor saxophone, clarinet

'Us and Them' revisited, but without the lyrics, melody, or dynamics. There is a nice solo, though, from British jazz saxophonist Gilad Atzmon, who had previously worked with Gilmour's friend Robert Wyatt.

'The Lost Art of Conversation'

Richard Wright: music, piano

Some pleasant piano from Richard Wright, which almost seems as though it might be going somewhere, but it does not.

'On Noodle Street'

David Gilmour: guitars
Richard Wright: keyboards
Nick Mason: percussion
Guy Pratt: bass
Jon Carin: keyboards

The presence of Guy Pratt and Jon Carin made this at least sound like an actual band performance, and Wright's electric piano from 'Sheep' makes a welcome re-appearance. However, this one-chord misfire outstays even its brief duration.

'Night Light'

David Gilmour: music, guitars
Richard Wright: music, keyboards
Nick Mason: percussion

Lots of echoing guitar, drawn out keyboards, and not much else.

'Allons-y (1)'

David Gilmour: music, guitars
Richard Wright: keyboards
Nick Mason: percussion
Bob Ezrin: bass
Jon Carin: keyboards, percussion loop

An attempt to inject some life into the somnambulism on show so far, it sounds a lot like 'Run Like Hell', but without the anger or urgency.

'Autumn '68'

Richard Wright: music, organ
Damon Iddins: keyboards

Ninety seconds on Wright noodling on a large organ in 1968 with 2014 overdubs. The song is actually quite nice, and would have fitted into the middle of, say, 'Echoes' or 'Atom Heart Mother'.

The title is a wry nod to 'Summer '68', Wright's song from *Atom Heart Mother*.

'Allons-y (2)'

David Gilmour: music, guitars
Richard Wright: keyboards
Nick Mason: percussion
Bob Ezrin: bass
Jon Carin: keyboards, percussion loop

An unwelcome reprise of 'Allons-y (1)', the title means 'Let's go'. Possibly ironically.

'Talkin' Hawkin''

David Gilmour: music, guitars

Richard Wright: music, keyboards
Nick Mason: percussion
Guy Pratt: bass
Durga McBroom: backing vocals

While this does sound like a real song played by a real band, with some restrained bass playing from Guy Pratt and 'oo-ahh' backing vocals, the song it sounds like is 'Keep Talking' from *The Division Bell*. This effect is compounded by including the same Stephen Hawking samples as its progenitor.

'Calling'

David Gilmour: music, guitars
Richard Wright: keyboards
Nick Mason: percussion
Anthony Moore: music, keyboards

One suspects that the only reason this aimless one-chord synthesiser track has been included is to provide some ready cash for cohort Anthony Moore, who is perhaps not living comfortably on all those Slapp Happy royalties.

'Eyes to Pearls'

David Gilmour: music, guitars
Richard Wright: keyboards
Nick Mason: percussion
Andy Jackson: bass

This is such an obvious rewrite of 'Set the Controls for the Heart of the Sun' that it is surprising Roger Waters has not sued.

'Surfacing'

David Gilmour: music, guitars
Richard Wright: keyboards
Nick Mason: percussion
Durga McBroom: backing vocals

The central section to 'Poles Apart', spruced up with some backing vocals. Probably the most successful piece on *The Endless River*, as Gilmour's slide guitar soars and sings.

'Louder than Words'

David Gilmour: music, guitars
Richard Wright: keyboards
Nick Mason: percussion
Bob Ezrin: bass
Durga McBroom: backing vocals
Louise Marshal: backing vocals
Sarah Brown: backing vocals
Chantal Leverton: viola
Victoria Lyon: violin
Helen Nash: cello
Honor Watson: violin
Polly Sampson: lyrics

If this whole album sounds like one (very) long introduction waiting for a song, then here, at last, is that song. It certainly sounds like Pink Floyd, but the asinine lyrics ('An old pair of shoes, your favourite blues, gonna tap out the rhythm / Let's go with the flow, wherever it goes') must have made old Roger Waters laugh into his whisky.

> I didn't necessarily always give [Richard Wright] his proper due. People have very different attitudes to the way they work and we can become very judgmental and think someone is not quite pulling his weight enough, without realising that theirs is a different weight to pull.
>
> David Gilmour, *The Guardian*, 9 October 2014

> The closing 'Louder than Words', has lyrics written by Gilmour's wife, Polly Samson, about bitching and fighting, making up and carrying on. It's quite fitting for a band that has had its fair share of conflict and turbulence.
>
> Molloy Woodcraft, *The Guardian*, 9 November 2014

> They don't do small talk, they don't do big talk. It's not hostile, they just don't speak.
>
> Polly Samson, *Entertainment Weekly* (16 September 2015)

> Richard Wright was the steady, binding majesty in the Floyd's explorations. This album is an unexpected, welcome epitaph.
>
> David Fricke, *Rolling Stone* (7 November 2014)

Extra Songs on the Deluxe Edition

'TBS9'

Written by David Gilmour and Richard Wright.

Part of the unreleased 'The Big Spliff' project, this is a reworking of 'Careful with That Axe, Eugene'.

'TBS14'

Written by David Gilmour and Richard Wright.

A piece deemed not good enough to be included on Pink Floyd's worst album? This is nothing more than a vague sketch of a half-finished idea, yet it lasts for over four minutes.

'Nervana'

Written by David Gilmour.

Gilmour thrashes away for nearly six minutes. Buyers of the deluxe edition must have been delighted.

Reviews

> It's just aimless jamming, one long thread of Dave Gilmour's guitar against Rick Wright's pastel keyboards and Nick Mason's tentative percussion, with nary a melody of any distinction alighted upon for the duration. All that's left is ghastly faux-psychedelic dinner-party muzak. Which is fine, if you're thinking of throwing a ghastly faux-psychedelic dinner-party.
>
> Andy Gill, *The Independent*, 5 November 2014

> This band always makes your speakers feel inadequate.
>
> Helen Brown, *The Telegraph*, 4 November 2014

> This is the last thing that'll be out from us. I'm pretty certain there will not be any follow up to this.
>
> David Gilmour, *The Guardian*, 9 October 2014

APPENDIX I

Solo Albums

Syd Barrett—*The Madcap Laughs* (January 1970)

A disjointed and quirkily enigmatic collection of cracked songs with many highlights.
Listen to: 'Octopus', 'Dark Globe'.

Ron Geesin and Roger Waters—*Music from the Body* (November 1970)

An avant-garde soundtrack album with some *Ummagumma* sound effects and acoustic songsmithery, and an uncredited Pink Floyd can be heard on 'Give Birth to a Smile'.
Listen to: 'Sea Shell and Stone', 'Give Birth to a Smile'.

Syd Barrett—*Barrett* (November 1970)

A quirky and disjointedly cracked collection of enigmatic songs with many highlights, produced by David Gilmour and Richard Wright.
Listen to: 'Dominoes', 'Gigolo Aunt'.

Syd Barrett—*Syd Barrett* (November 1974)

A double album, collating both of Barrett's two solo albums.

David Gilmour—*David Gilmour* (May 1978)

An uninspired, if pleasant, collection of low-key songs.
Listen to: 'There's No Way Out Of Here', 'I Can't Breathe Any More'.

Richard Wright—*Wet Dream* (May 1978)

A pleasant, if uninspired, collection of low-key songs.
Listen to: 'Against the Odds'.

Nick Mason's Fictitious Sports—*Nick Mason's Fictitious Sports* (May 1981)

Essentially a Carla Bley solo album with Robert Wyatt singing.
Listen to: 'Hot River'.

David Gilmour—*About Face* (March 1984)

A mixed bag of '80s sounds with some good songs and the occasional angsty bite.
Listen to: 'Murder', 'All Lovers are Deranged', 'Near the End'.

Zee—*Identity* (April 1984)

Rick Wright fails to break his creative hiatus, despite assistance from Dee Harris.
Listen to: 'Confusion'.

Roger Waters—*The Pros and Cons of Hitch Hiking* (April 1984)

An intermittently entertaining dream-song cycle, with some tremendous guitar playing from Eric Clapton.
Listen to: 'Sexual Revolution', 'Every Stranger's Eyes'.

Mason + Fenn—*Profiles* (July 1985)

A forgettable '80s snore-fest, with Gilmour singing on one track.
Listen to: 'Lie for a Lie'.

Roger Waters—*When the Wind Blows* (May 1986)

Two pretty good songs and lots of noodling. From the soundtrack of the animated movie of Raymond Briggs' chilling graphic novel.
Listen to: 'Towers of Faith', 'Folded Flags'.

Syd Barrett—*The Peel Session* (January 1987)

Five songs recorded for the BBC in 1970, one unavailable elsewhere.
Listen to: 'Two of a Kind'.

Mason + Fenn—*White of the Eye* (January 1987)

Wholly instrumental soundtrack for a low-key British thriller starring David Keith and Cathy Moriarty.

Roger Waters—*Radio KAOS* (June 1987)

Confusing and over-produced political satire with an uplifting conclusion.
Listen to: 'The Powers That Be', 'Who Needs Information?', 'The Tide is Turning'

Syd Barrett—*Opel* (October 1988)

A compilation of unreleased material and alternate takes of recordings from sessions for Barrett's two solo albums. No sign of 'Bob Dylan Blues', however.
Listen to: 'Milky Way'.

Mason-Fenn—*Tank Malling* (December 1989)

Mostly instrumental soundtrack for a low-key British thriller starring Ray Winstone and Amanda Donahoe.

Roger Waters—*The Wall – Live in Berlin* (August 1990)

An audio documentation of a multi-guested Berlin performance.
Listen to: 'Young Lust', 'Comfortably Numb', 'The Tide is Turning'.

Syd Barrett—*Octopus* (May 1992)

A best-of with tracks from *The Madcap Laughs*, *Barrett*, and *Opel*. There is still no 'Bob Dylan's Blues', though.

Roger Waters—*Amused to Death* (September 1992)

An unexpectedly outstanding album with many highlights, and, for once, music and lyrics in perfect balance. In addition, there is sparkling guitar from Jeff Beck. Waters' best solo work by miles, especially the closing twenty minutes, which equals any of his work with Pink Floyd.
Listen to: 'Perfect Sense', 'Watching TV', 'It's a Miracle', 'Amused to Death'.

Syd Barrett—*Crazy Diamond* (April 1993)

Box set of *The Madcap Laughs* (with six bonus tracks), *Barrett* (with seven bonus tracks), and *Opel* (with six bonus tracks). Still no 'Bob Dylan's Blues'.

Richard Wright—*Broken China* (November 1996)

Rick Wright's concept album about his wife's battle with depression. It is beautifully performed and produced, but not particularly engaging.

Listen to: 'Night of a Thousand Furry Toys', 'Breakthrough'.

Roger Waters—*In the Flesh* (December 2000)

A pointless but well-recorded concert souvenir with one new song.
Listen to: 'Each Small Candle'.

Syd Barrett—*Wouldn't You Miss Me* (April 2001)

A best-of with tracks from *The Madcap Laughs*, *Barrett*, *Opel*, and *The Peel Sessions*, plus one unheard song.
Listen to: 'Bob Dylan's Blues'.

Roger Waters—*Flickering Flame* (May 2002)

A greatest hits compilation with some dull new songs.
Listen to: 'Knockin' on Heaven's Door', 'Flickering Flame', 'Lost Boys Calling'.

Syd Barrett—*Radio One Sessions* (March 2004)

A re-release of *The Peel Sessions* with three songs from *Sounds of the Seventies* in 1971.

Roger Waters—'To Kill the Child'/'Leaving Beirut' (2004)

An intriguing single-only release.

Roger Waters—*Ça Ira* (September 2005)

Waters' long-awaited opera.
Listen to: something else.

David Gilmour—*On An Island* (March 2006)

Flaccid. Lyrics by wife. A big success.
Listen to: 'On an Island', 'The Blue'.

David Gilmour—'Arnold Layne' (December 2006)

A CD single with two live versions of Pink Floyd's debut single, one sung by David Bowie.

Roger Waters—'Hello, I Love You' (2007)

Not The Doors song, this is from the soundtrack to *The Last Mimzy*.

David Gilmour—*Live in Gdańsk* (September 2008)

An intermittently successful live album that injects some life into the *On an Island* songs and delivers a robust version of 'Echoes'.

Listen to: 'Echoes', 'Coming Back to Life'.

Syd Barrett—*An Introduction to Syd Barrett* (April 2010)

Finally Syd Barrett get the compilation he deserves, with his best group and solo work remastered and, in some cases, remixed by David Gilmour. There is even a new mix of the alternative version of 'Matilda Mother' that was first heard on the 40th anniversary edition of *Piper at the Gates of Dawn*—and 'Bob Dylan Blues'.

The Orb featuring David Gilmour—*Metallic Spheres* (October 2010)

Superior ambient noodling.

Listen to: 'Hymns to the Sun'.

Roger Waters—'We Shall Overcome' (2007)

A non-album single.

David Gilmour—*Rattle That Lock* (September 2015)

An improvement on his previous solo album.

Listen to: 'In Any Tongue'.

Roger Waters—*Roger Waters: The Wall* (November 2015)

A pointless but well-recorded concert souvenir with one new song.

Listen to: 'The Ballad of Jean Charles de Menezes'.

Roger Waters—*Is This the Life We Really Want* (June 2017)

Waters' first album of new music since 1992. With perhaps too much finger-pointing from rock's last angry man, overall, this is a welcome return to form, uplifting and emotion in equal measure.

Listen to: 'The Last Refugee', 'Picture That', 'Déjà Vu'

APPENDIX II

Videos and DVDs

Live at Pompeii (September 1972)

Pink Floyd perform without an audience in the amphitheatre in Pompeii and in a studio in Paris. Undeniably impressive.

Pink Floyd—The Wall (August 1982)

A visual representation of Roger Waters' bleak album. Miserable and depressing throughout, but with stunning animations and many reworked songs. Buy the DVD for Waters' fabulous commentary.

The Final Cut (1983)

Surprisingly moving visuals to four songs from one of Pink Floyd's most underrated albums.

Delicate Sound of Thunder (June 1989)

A standard in-concert performance of the 1988 set.

La Carrera Panamericana (June 1992)

A documentary in which we follow Gilmour, Mason and manager Steve O'Rourke in a car race across Mexico. Pink Floyd provide some new, fairly mundane, music recorded at Olympic Studios in November 1991: 'Country Theme' (Gilmour); 'Small Theme' (Gilmour); 'Big Theme' (Gilmour); 'Carrera Slow Blues' (Gilmour/Wright/Mason); 'Mexico '78' (Gilmour); 'Pan Am Shuffle' (Gilmour/Wright/Mason).

P•U•L•S•E (June 1995 (VHS), July 2006 (DVD))

A standard in-concert performance of the 1994 *Dark Side* set. There are many mildly diverting extras on the DVD.

The Pink Floyd and Syd Barrett Story (March 2003)

A superb BBC documentary, featuring new interviews with Waters, Gilmour, Wright and Mason.

The Making of The Dark Side of the Moon (August 2003)

A fascinating documentary with lots of good material and new interviews with Waters, Gilmour, Wright and Mason—plus mesmerising segments with Alan Parsons dissecting the master tapes. Includes solo acoustic versions of 'Brain Damage' and 'Money' performed by Roger Waters, a solo acoustic performance of 'Breathe' by David Gilmour, and the original demo recordings of 'Time' and 'Money'.

The Story of Wish You Were Here (June 2012)

An equally well-produced 'making of', featuring new interviews with Waters, Gilmour and Mason, as well as many other participants. Engineer Brian Humphries plays back some of the original sound tapes from Abbey Road Studios archives.

The Early Years 1965–1972 (November 2016)

A massively comprehensive box set with extensive video material.

Promo films:

'Arnold Layne' (1967)
'Arnold Layne' (alternative version) (1967)
'Jugband Blues' (1967)
'Point Me at the Sky' (1968)

TV broadcasts:

'Interstellar Overdrive' from *Scene—Underground* (London, 1967)
'Pow R. Toc H.' and 'Astronomy Domine', plus interviews with Syd Barrett and Roger Waters, from BBC's *The Look Of The Week* (London, 1967)
'The Scarecrow' from *Pathé Pictorial* (1967)
'Apples & Oranges' plus a Dick Clark interview (Los Angeles, 1967)

'Instrumental Improvisation' from BBC *Tomorrow's World* (London, 1967)
'See Emily Play' from BBC *Top of the Pops* (London, 1967)
'Apples and Oranges' from *Vibrato* (Brussels, 1968)
'Astronomy Domine', 'Flaming', 'Set the Controls for the Heart Of the Sun', and 'Let There Be More Light' from *Bouton Rouge* (Paris, 1968)
'Paintbox' from *Discorama* (Paris, 1968)
'Instrumental Improvisation' from *The Sound of Change* (London, 1968)
'Set the Controls for the Heart Of the Sun' from *All My Loving* (London, 1968)
'It Would Be So Nice (excerpt)' from *Release-Rome Goes Pop* (April 1968)
'Interstellar Overdrive' from *Pop 68* (Rome, 1968)
'Astronomy Domine' and Roger Waters interview from *Tienenklanken—Kastival* (Belgium, 1968)
'Let There Be More Light' and 'Remember a Day' from *Samedi et Compagnie* (Paris, 1968)
'Let There Be More Light' from *A L'Affiche du Monde* (London, 1968)
'Let There Be More Light' and 'Flaming' from *Tous En Scene* (Paris, 1968)
'Let There Be More Light' from *Surprise Partie* (Paris, 1968)
'Corporal Clegg', band interview, and 'A Saucerful of Secrets' from *P1–P wie Petersilie* (Stuggart, 1969)
'Atom Heart Mother', 'Cymbaline', 'Grantchester Meadows', 'Green Is the Colour', 'Careful With That Axe, Eugene' and 'Set The Controls For The Heart Of The Sun' from *An Hour with Pink Floyd*, KQED, San Francisco, USA, 30 April 1970
Interview and 'Atom Heart Mother (extracts)' from *Aspekte* (Hamburg, 1971)
'Careful With That Axe, Eugene' and band interview from *Get To Know* (Sydney, Australia, 1971)
Recording *Obscured by Clouds*, plus David Gilmour and Roger Waters interview, from *Pop Deux* (1972)
Roland Petit Pink Floyd Ballet, France, news reports, from *Actualités Méditerranée*, (Marseille, 1972), *JT Nuit – Les Pink Floyd* (Marseille, 1972), *JT 20h – Pink Floyd* (Paris, 1973), *Journal de Paris – Les Pink Floyd* (Paris, 1973) and *Autour Du Passage Des Pink Floyd* (Poitiers, 1972)

Live material:

'Instrumental Improvisation' (London, 1967)
'Interstellar Overdrive' (London, 1967)
'Astronomy Domine', 'The Scarecrow', 'Corporal Clegg', 'Paintbox', 'Set The Controls For The Heart Of The Sun', 'See Emily Play' and 'Bike' (Tienerklanken, Brussels, Belgium, 18–19 February 1968)
'Set the Controls for the Heart of the Sun', 'A Saucerful of Secrets' and David Gilmour interview (Forum Musiques, Paris, France, 22 January 1969)
'Careful With That Axe, Eugene' and 'A Saucerful Of Secrets' (Essencer Pop & Blues Festival, Essen, Germany, 11 October 1969)

'Green is the Colour', 'Careful with That Axe, Eugene' and 'Set the Controls for the Heart of the Sun' (Music Power & European Music Revolution, Festival Actuel Amougies Mont de LÉnclus, Belgium, 25 October 1969)
'Atom Heart Mother' (Bath Festival of Blues & Progressive Music, Shepton Mallet, UK, 27 June 1970)
'Set the Controls for the Heart of the Sun' and 'A Saucerful Of Secrets' (Kralingen Music Festival, Rotterdam, 28 June 1970)
'Atom Heart Mother' (Hyde Park, London, UK, 18 July 1970)
'Cymbaline' (sound check), 'Atom Heart Mother', 'Embryo', 'Green Is The Colour', 'Careful With That Axe, Eugene' and 'Set The Controls For The Heart Of The Sun' (Pop Deux Festival de St. Tropez, France, 8 August 1970)
'Instrumental Improvisations' and 'Embryo' from Roland Petit Ballet, Paris, France, 5 December 1970
'A Saucerful Of Secrets (extract)' (Offenbach, Germany, 26 February 1971)
'Set the Control for the Heart of the Sun' and 'Cymbaline' (Cinq Grands Sur La Deux, Abbaye de Royaumont, Asnierès-sur-Oise, France, 15 June 1971)
'Atom Heart Mother (extracts)' (Musikforum Ossiachersee, Ossiach, Austria, 1971)
'Atom Heart Mother' ('71 Hakone Aphrodite Open Air Festival, Hakone, Japan, 6–7 August 1971)
'Atom Heart Mother', 'Careful with That Axe, Eugene' and 'A Saucerful of Secrets' (The Amsterdam Rock Circus, 22 May 1972)
'Set The Controls For The Heart Of The Sun' and 'Careful With That Axe, Eugene' (Brighton Dome, 29 June 1972)

Documentary material:

'Chapter 24' at EMI Studios, London, 1967
Recording 'Interstellar Overdrive' and 'Nick's Boogie', London, 1967
'The Scarecrow (outtakes)' from *Pathé Pictorial* (1967)
'Afternoon' ('Biding My Time'), 'The Beginning' ('Green is the Colour'), 'Cymbaline', 'Beset by Creatures of the Deep' ('Careful with That Axe, Eugene') and 'The End of the Beginning' ('A Saucerful of Secrets')—*The Man and the Journey* rehearsals, Royal Festival Hall, London, rehearsal, April 1969
'Interstellar Overdrive' (with Frank Zappa)
Pink Floyd and Steve O'Rourke, from 24 hours – Bootleg Records, London, 1971
Storm Thorgerson and Aubrey 'Po' Powell interviewed, from *Review*, London, 1971
'One of These Days' - Ian Emes animation, created July 1972
Recording *Obscured by Clouds*, Château d'Hérouville, France, 23–29 February 1972
'Careful With That Axe, Eugene', 'A Saucerful Of Secrets', 'One Of These Days', 'Set The Controls For The Heart Of The Sun' and 'Echoes', *Live At Pompeii* 2016 5.1 Audio Remix

Feature films with Pink Floyd soundtracks:

The Committee
More
La Vallée (*Obscured by Clouds*)

Endnotes

Chapter 1

1. Cliff Jones in *Echoes: The Stories Behind Every Pink Floyd Song* (1996).
2. Mark Blake in *Pigs Might Fly: The Inside Story of Pink Floyd* (2007)
3. The B-side of 'See Emily Play' was 'The Scarecrow', released on *The Piper at the Gates of Dawn* and discussed in that section.
4. The US release omitted 'Astronomy Domine', 'Flaming', and 'Bike', but added 'See Emily Play'. The US re-release for *A Nice Pair* (5 December 1973) utilised the *Ummagumma* version of 'Astronomy Domine', the single mix of 'Flaming', and the *Relics* mix of 'Bike'.
5. This author does not agree with the many music journalists who cite Syd Barrett as the only major musical force in Pink Floyd. This myth has a dual source: firstly, Barrett's well-documented mental breakdown (therefore he ceased performing at a perceived peak of creativity and didn't make an ill-advised comeback in the 1980s), and secondly the inverted snobbery against anything that sells in volume, starting with *The Dark Side of the Moon*. Waters, Gilmour, and Wright should share the kudos as the joint musical architects of Pink Floyd's most enduring work, all created between 1970 and 1977, with nods to Barrett's undoubted genius in 1967, Waters' flashes of inspiration in 1979–1983 and Gilmour's occasional flourish in the post-Waters years.
6. Pronounced doh-me-nay, not doh-meen or doh-mine.
7. Some sources place this as being recorded at Thompson Private Recorders in Hemel Hempstead in November 1966.
8. Along with 'Scarecrow', 'Chapter 24', 'Careful with That Axe, Eugene', 'Grantchester Meadows', 'Atom Heart Mother', 'If', 'Fat Old Sun', 'Fearless', 'San Tropez', 'Breathe', 'Brain Damage', 'Eclipse', 'Dogs', 'Mother', 'Young Lust', 'Nobody Home', 'Your Possible Pasts', 'The Gunner's Dream' and 'Paranoid Eyes'. As listed by James Guthrie on www.pinkfloyd.co.uk
9. David Bowie's own gnome song, 'The Laughing Gnome', was recorded concurrently with *The Piper at the Gates of Dawn* and released as a single on 14 April 1967. Unlike Pink Floyd's song, Bowie's bears repeated listening.

10. John Peel announces the song as 'The Massed Gadgets of Hercules', which is odd considering the album of which this song forms a part would be released the following week.
11. Quoted in *Crazy Diamond—Syd Barrett and the Dawn of Pink Floyd* (Mike Watkinson, 1991)

Chapter 2

1. Archive recordings from 1967, 1968, 1969, 1970, 1971, 1974, and 1980–81 have subsequently been made available, along with contemporary live albums from 1988, 1990, and 1994.
2. The guitar was bought by Gilmour from Manny's Music in New York City, probably in the last week of May 1970. Pink Floyd had performed at the Fillmore East in New York City on 9 and 16 April 1970, but all of their stage equipment was stolen after a gig in New Orleans on 16 May, prematurely ending their tour. Presumably Gilmour visited Manny's to buy a replacement on the way back to London via New York.
3. For the full, unexpurgated, and frequently hilarious story of Ron Geesin's relationship with Pink Floyd, I recommend his excellent book *The Flaming Cow: The Making of Pink Floyd's Atom Heart Mother* (2013).
4. One song, 'Give Birth to a Smile', was recorded by the full Pink Floyd line-up.
5. Roger Waters' prominent bass line in 'Funky Dung' is note-for-note the same as part of the bass arrangements on the *Ummagumma* version of 'Careful with That Axe, Eugene', and both 'Explosion' and 'Unknown Song (Rain in the Country)' from *Zabriskie Point*.
6. There has been discussion about where exactly these sections start and end. The timings included here are taken from *The Flaming Cow: The Making of Pink Floyd's Atom Heart Mother* (2013) by Ron Geesin, and are therefore unarguably correct.
7. In Bath, the piece was announced as 'The Amazing Pudding'. Pink Floyd are known to have performed 'Atom Heart Mother' with brass and choir a total of nineteen times.
8. Gilmour's remarkable guitar solo in the version recorded at the Royal Albert Hall in May 2006 (available on the *Remember That Night* DVD) is as good as any other in his long career.
9. Some sources spell his surname as Stiles.

Chapter 3

1. Even better when you can see how he does it in the *Live at Pompeii* film, especially his smart recovery after losing a drumstick mere seconds before a key drum fill.
2. Waters is a devout Arsenal fan.
3. 'Seamus' was remade as 'Mademoiselle Nobs', featuring a different dog and no lyrics, in the film *Pink Floyd: Live at Pompeii* (recorded in Studio Europasonor, Paris, from 13–20 December 1972 but, for some reason, not released as an audio track with the rest of the sessions on the otherwise exhaustive *The Early Years 1965–1972*).
4. This is the definitive version of this track, in my view, and was very obviously not recorded outdoors in an ancient Roman amphitheatre.
5. This completes the set list from this historic show, as set one is available on the *Experience* and *Immersion* box sets of *Wish You Were Here*, and set two on the *Experience* and *Immersion* box sets of *The Dark Side of the Moon*. The 1974 version of 'Echoes' is unique in that it includes lush, gospel backing vocals from Venetta Fields and Carlena Williams, and a fruity saxophone solo by Dick Parry. After contending with years of rough-sounding bootleg recordings of the 1974 tour, we should be grateful that someone in the Floyd organisation had the foresight to include this terrific recording on *The Early Years* box set, even if fans needed to re-mortgage their houses to afford to buy it.
6. All date from the first half of 1972: 'Burning Bridges' and 'Stay' from *Obscured by Clouds*, and the already-written but not-yet-recorded 'Us and Them'.
7. Manning quote from *The Rough Guide to Pink Floyd* (2006)
8. Thomas, who had worked for The Beatles, Procol Harum and John Cage, would later produce Roxy Music, the Sex Pistols, INXS, The Pretenders, Elton John, Pulp, and Paul McCartney amongst many others.
9. John Harris in *The Dark Side of the Moon: The Making of Pink Floyd's Masterpiece* suggests that the opening chords in 'Breathe' 'may or may not have been pilfered from Neil Young's 'Down by the River''. Em7 to A chord changes are very common, as both chords are physically and harmonically related.
10. A live version from 1972 is on the *Experience* and *Discovery* versions of *The Dark Side of the Moon* (2011).
11. Released in 2011 on the *Experience* and *Discovery* versions of *The Dark Side of the Moon* (2011).
12. For the record, the full list is Freddie Mercury (Queen), 'Bohemian Rhapsody'; Clare Torry (Pink Floyd), 'The Great Gig in the Sky'; John Lennon (The Beatles), 'Twist and Shout'; Roger Daltrey (The Who), 'Love Reign O'er Me'; Tina Turner (Ike and Tina Turner), 'River Deep, Mountain High'; Robert Plant (Led Zeppelin), 'Stairway to Heaven'; Merry Clayton (The Rolling Stones), 'Gimme Shelter'; Ian Gillan (Deep Purple), 'Child in Time'; Kurt Cobain (Nirvana), 'Where Did You Sleep Last Night?'; and Joe Cocker, 'With a Little Help From My Friends'

13. She also performed the song several times on Roger Water's 1987 solo tour.
14. Released 12 May 1973.
15. Gilmour would later learn the alto saxophone, performing a sax-led instrumental on his 2006 solo album *On an Island*.
16. John Harris suggests that the live debut of 'Eclipse' was at Leicester De Montford Hall on 10 February 1972.
17. A similarly pointless endeavour coloured early sessions for *Meddle* in 1971.
18. 'The Hard Way' was released on the *Immersion* box set of *The Dark Side of the Moon* (2011); 'Glasses' was released on the *Experience* and *Immersion* box set versions of *Wish You Were Here* (2011).
19. Live versions from 17 November 1974 are available on the *Experience* and *Immersion* box set versions of *Wish You Were Here* (2011). Many of the most die-hard fans would have first owned these three songs on the famous *Winter Tour '74* bootleg recorded 19 November 1974. It is said that this sold over 10,000 copies in 1975.
20. A full-length version can be heard on the bootleg album *From Abbey Road to Britannia Row—The Extraction Tapes*, along with alternative mixes of 'Welcome to the Machine' and 'Have a Cigar'.
21. As quoted in the radio series *Shades of Pink: The Definitive Pink Floyd Profile* (1984)
22. An early mix of the song omits the acoustic guitar in favour of some Gilmour voice-box electric lead, used to superb effect in 'Sheep', which was recorded the following year.
23. David Gilmour returned the favour, adding a stinging lead guitar solo to Harper's song 'The Game', released on the album *HQ* recorded at EMI in March 1975 and released three months later. Gilmour would also guest on Harper's albums *The Unknown Solider* (1980) and *Once* (1990). A version of 'Have a Cigar' with vocals by both Waters and Gilmour can be heard on the *Experience* and *Immersion* box set versions of *Wish You Were Here* (2011). Sometimes listed as a duet, it is more likely two separate vocal tracks over the same backing track.
24. Both Waters and Gilmour have performed most or some of this second section in their own concerts. Waters included Parts VI and VII (and a short reprise of Part I) in his 1999–2002 concert repertoire, available on the CD/DVD *In the Flesh*. Gilmour included Parts VI and VII in his London and Paris concerts in 2001, available on the DVD *David Gilmour in Concert*.

Chapter 4

1. Parts of *The Wall*, including the children's choir in 'Another Brick in the Wall, Part 2', would be recorded at Britannia Row.
2. Live versions would be performed by the whole band, not just by Waters alone, and conclude with a solo played by Floyd auxiliary Snowy White. White performed with Pink Floyd on their 1977 and 1980 tour dates, played on Richard

Wright's 1978 solo album and is a long-time member of Roger Waters' Bleeding Heart Band (since 1999). His 1983 solo song 'Bird of Paradise' was a UK Top 10 hit single and he has released many albums under his own name, as well as two as a member of Thin Lizzy.

3. Joe is the correct name, according to Vernon Fitch—not Ron DiBlasi as used in many sources.
4. *UK Business Insider*, 23 September 2016
5. 'In the Flesh' and several of the other songs on the original studio album were remixed and/or re-recorded for the soundtrack of the film *Pink Floyd – The Wall* released in July 1982. Some of these are significantly different. Specifically, 'In the Flesh' was re-recorded and extended; 'The Thin Ice' was remixed and extended; 'Another Brick in the Wall, Part 2' is remixed with additional lead guitar; 'Mother' was partially rerecorded with some different lyrics; 'Goodbye Blue Sky' and 'The Trial' were remixed; 'Don't Leave Me Now' and 'Run Like Hell' were edited and remixed; 'Another Brick in the Wall, Part 3', 'Outside the Wall' and 'In The Flesh' were re-recorded, the latter with Bob Geldof's lead vocals.
6. The 2012 box set of *The Wall* includes extracts from many of Waters' home demos. Those that do not appear in this format in this box set are: 'The Thin Ice', 'Another Brick in the Wall, Part 1', 'The Happiest Days of Our Lives', and 'The Show Must Go On'. This suggests that these songs were written once the project moved into the full band phase—but the Waters demos publicly released may, of course, be incomplete.
7. The original titles for Parts I to III were 'Reminiscing', 'Education', and 'Drugs'.
8. 'Mother' received extensive overdubs in Los Angeles on 1, 12, and 15 October 1979.
9. The 'second band demo' of 'Mother' on the box set is identical to the first, but with added keyboards.
10. The chorus lyrics of 'Comfortably Numb' never changed through the various rewrites of the song during 1979.
11. This timing is taken from *The Wall* CD and includes twenty-nine seconds of sound effects before the song begins.
12. Waters' vocalists for his solo shows have included Van Morrison, Rick Danko and Levon Helm (1990), Bruce Hornsby (1991), Don Henley (1992 and 2002), Doyle Bramhall II (1999–2000), Chester Kamen (2002), Jon Carin and Andy Fairweather-Low (2006–2007), Eddie Vedder (2012), and Robbie Wyckoff (2010–2013, 2016). Those taking on Gilmour's iconic solo include Snowy White (1990–2016), Rick Di Fonzo (1990), Doyle Bramhall II (1999–2000), Chester Kamen (2002), and Dave Kilminster (2006–2007, 2010–2013, 2016). The vocalists on David Gilmour's solo tours have been Gregg Dechert and Mickey Feat (1984), Robert Wyatt (2001), Bob Geldof (2002), Kate Bush (2002), Durga McBroom (2002), David Bowie (2006), Richard Wright (2006), Jon Carin (2016), and Greg Phillinganes (2016).

13. Also on Gilmour's contributions to the songs 'True Story' on Roy Harper's album *The Unknown Soldier* (1980) and 'Give Blood' on Pete Townshend's *White City* (1985).
14. Newmark would tour as a member of Waters' solo band in 1984–1985 and performs on Gilmour's album *On an Island,* released in 2006.
15. In *Pigs Might Fly: The Inside Story of Pink Floyd* (2007)
16. I first heard *The Final Cut* as an impressionable 16-year-old when it was released in spring 1983. I suspect that this album, more than any other influence, prompted me to become a writer. So now you know who to blame.
17. Chris Ott, *Pitchfork Media*
18. Listen to his commentary on the DVD of Alan Parson's film *The Wall.* He really is hilarious.
19. Mason also relinquished his drumming duties to another session player, Jeff Porcaro, on the equally complex 'Mother' from *The Wall.*

Chapter 5

1. According to a 2011 interview with Pink Floyd's engineer Andy Jackson, a 'new' version of *A Momentary Lapse of Reason* could be released one day. These quotes are from an interview with SuperDeluxeEdition.com in July 2011:

   > SDE: Will *A Momentary Lapse of Reason* be remixed for an Immersion box set? David Gilmour has mentioned before his interest in 'mixing the 80s out of it'.
   >
   > AJ: Interesting point. *A Momentary Lapse of Reason* is an odd one out inasmuch as it's the only album that was trying to be 'of the time', which now means it sounds dated, rather than timeless. We have started this process a while ago, doing new drums with Nick with a much more 'Pink Floyd classic' approach. If and when we'll pick it up I don't know.
   >
   > SDE: One assumes that if there was to be an Immersion Edition of *A Momentary Lapse of Reason* then this process would probably be completed. Is it just the drums that have been redone so far?
   >
   > AJ: Yes and yes. It was our intention to remove some of the 80's synths and get more Rick Hammond on it. Obviously not possible for him to do it now, but we started the process of pulling some of his playing from gigs of those songs. Just a lot of editing/syncing to do on that, but it should work.

2. The edited single version begins with the first drum hit (the 'clocks noises' part of the album version is skipped). The rototom intro is edited and does not have the background keyboards. The central part with bass solo is edited, the last chorus is repeated and the song fades out much earlier.

3. In his exhaustingly detailed *The Pink Floyd Encyclopaedia* (3rd edition, 2005)
4. The single has edits during the piano/bells intro, the central instrumental section, and during the lap steel solo, reducing it from 8:31 to 5:13 in length.
5. Floyd fans should seek out the DVD *The Strat Pack: Live in Concert,* a film of a September 2004 concert during which Gilmour performs a jaw-dropping version of 'Marooned', as well as two other latter-day Floyd songs.
6. An unofficial fan remix double CD released as *Forever and Ever* mixes *The Endless River* outtakes throughout *The Division Bell*—'Surfacing' is reinserted into 'Poles Apart', for example, and 'Talkin' Hawkin'' sits comfortably as a coda to 'Keep Talking'. Surprisingly this manages to improve both albums immeasurably and results in a genuinely uplifting listen.

Bibliography

Blake, M., *Pigs Might Fly: The Inside Story of Pink Floyd* (London; Aurum Press, 2007, updated 2013, published as *Comfortably Numb* in the US)

Christgau, R., *Christgau's Record Guide - 1970s* (New York; Mariner Books, 1981)

Du Noyer, P., *In The City* (London; Virgin Books, 2009)

Fitch, V., *The Pink Floyd Encyclopaedia* (3rd edition) (Pataskala, Ohio; CG Publishing, 2005)

Fitch, V., *Pink Floyd: The Press Reports 1966-1983* (Pataskala, Ohio; CG Publishing, 2001)

Geesin, R., *The Flaming Cow: The Making of Pink Floyd's Atom Heart Mother* (Stroud; The History Press, 2013)

Harris, J., *The Dark Side of the Moon: The Making of Pink Floyd's Masterpiece* (Glasgow; HarperCollins, 2005)

Heylin, C., *The Great White Wonders: A History of Rock Bootlegs* (London; Penguin, 1995)

Jones, C., *Echoes, the Stories Behind Every Pink Floyd Song* (London; Omnibus, 1996)

MacDonald, I., *Revolution in the Head* (London; Pimlico, 1994, updated 1998)

Manning, T., *The Rough Guide to Pink Floyd* (London; Rough Guides, 2006)

Mason, N., *Inside Out: A Personal History of Pink Floyd* (London; Weidenfeld & Nicolson, 2004, updated 2005)

Povey, G., *Echoes: The Complete History of Pink Floyd* (Bovingdon; Mind Head Publishing, 2007)

Peel, J., *The Olivetti Chronicles* (London; Bantam Press, 2008)

Pratt, G., *My Bass and Other Animals* (London; Orion, 2007)

Radcliffe, M., *Reelin' In the Years* (London; Simon & Schuster, 2011)

Rose, P., *Which One's Pink: Towards an Analysis of the Concept Albums of Roger Waters and Pink Floyd* (Hamilton, Ontario; McMaster University, 1995)

Schaffner, N., *A Saucerful of Secrets - The Pink Floyd Odyssey* (London; Sidgewick and Jackson, 1991)

Taylor, P., *The Black Strat* (Milwaukee, Wisconsin; Hal Leonard, 2008)